comforting casseroles

Easy Chicken & Biscuits

- **1 can (10¾ ounces) CAMPBELL'S® Condensed Cream of Celery Soup (Regular or 98% Fat Free)**
- **1 can (10¾ ounces) CAMPBELL'S® Condensed Cream of Potato Soup**
- **1 cup milk**
- **¼ teaspoon dried thyme leaves, crushed**
- **¼ teaspoon ground black pepper**
- **4 cups cooked cut-up vegetables (broccoli flowerets, cauliflower flowerets and/or carrots)**
- **2 cups cubed cooked chicken**
- **1 package (about 7 ounces) refrigerated buttermilk biscuits (10)**

1. Stir the soups, milk, thyme, black pepper, vegetables and chicken in a 13×9×2-inch shallow baking dish.

2. Bake at 400°F. for 15 minutes. Stir.

3. Cut each biscuit into quarters. Arrange cut biscuits over the chicken mixture.

4. Bake for 15 minutes more or until the biscuits are golden.   *Makes 5 servings*

Prep Time: 10 minutes
Bake Time: 30 minutes

Mediterranean Chicken & Bean Casserole

8 (2½ pounds) small chicken thighs
2 tablespoons all-purpose flour
1 teaspoon dried rosemary, crushed
1 teaspoon garlic salt
½ teaspoon black pepper
2 tablespoons olive oil
1 can (16 ounces) cannellini or Great Northern beans, drained
1 can (14½ ounces) diced tomatoes, undrained
8 slices SARGENTO® Deli Style Sliced Provolone or Mozzarella Cheese

REMOVE and discard skin and visible fat from chicken thighs. Rinse chicken in cold water; pat dry with paper towel. Combine flour, rosemary, garlic salt and pepper in plastic bag; add chicken to bag several pieces at a time, shaking to coat.

HEAT oil in large skillet over medium heat. Add chicken; cook 5 minutes per side or until golden brown. Transfer chicken to a 13×9-inch baking dish or 3-quart casserole. Drizzle pan juices over chicken. Combine beans and tomatoes; spoon over chicken. Cover dish with foil.

BAKE in a preheated 375°F oven 35 minutes or until chicken is no longer pink in center. Uncover; top chicken and bean mixture with cheese. Return to oven; bake, uncovered, 3 minutes or until cheese is melted.   *Makes 4 servings*

Prep Time: 20 minutes
Cook Time: 48 minutes

Chicken Scampi and Rice Bake

1 can (10¾ ounces) CAMPBELL'S® Condensed Cream of Chicken Soup (Regular or 98% Fat Free)

1⅓ cups water

2 tablespoons lemon juice

3 cloves garlic, minced *or* ¾ teaspoon garlic powder

¾ cup uncooked regular long-grain white rice

4 skinless, boneless chicken breast halves

2 slices lemon, cut in half

1. Stir the soup, water, lemon juice, garlic and rice in an 11×8-inch (2-quart) shallow baking dish. Top with the chicken. **Cover.**

2. Bake at 400°F. for 40 minutes or until the chicken is cooked through. Stir the mixture before serving. Garnish with lemon.   *Makes 4 servings*

Prep Time: 10 minutes
Bake Time: 40 minutes

tip

Long-grain rice kernels are four to five times longer than they are wide with tapered ends. They are lower in starch than shorter-grained kernels, resulting in a less sticky finished product.

Cajun Chicken and Rice

4 chicken drumsticks, skin removed
4 chicken thighs, skin removed
2 teaspoons Cajun seasoning
¾ teaspoon salt
2 tablespoons vegetable oil
1 can (about 14 ounces) chicken broth
1 cup uncooked rice
1 medium green bell pepper, coarsely chopped
1 medium red bell pepper, coarsely chopped
½ cup finely chopped green onions
2 cloves garlic, minced
½ teaspoon dried thyme
¼ teaspoon ground turmeric

1. Preheat oven to 350°F. Lightly coat 13×9-inch baking dish with nonstick cooking spray.

2. Pat chicken dry. Sprinkle both sides with Cajun seasoning and salt. Heat oil in large skillet over medium-high heat. Add chicken; cook 8 to 10 minutes or until browned on all sides. Transfer to plate.

3. Add broth to skillet. Bring to a boil, scraping browned bits from bottom of skillet. Add rice, peppers, green onions, garlic, thyme and turmeric; stir well. Pour into prepared baking dish. Place chicken on top. Cover tightly with foil. Bake 1 hour or until chicken is cooked through (165°F).

Makes 6 servings

Tomato-Topped Chicken & Stuffing

5 cups PEPPERIDGE FARM® Cubed Herb Seasoned Stuffing

6 tablespoons butter or margarine, melted

1¼ cups boiling water

4 skinless, boneless chicken breast halves

1 can (10¾ ounces) CAMPBELL'S® Condensed Cream of Chicken Soup (Regular or 98% Fat Free)

⅓ cup milk

1 medium tomato, sliced

1. Coarsely crush **1 cup** of the stuffing. Mix crushed stuffing with **2 tablespoons** of the butter in a small bowl. Set aside.

2. Mix the remaining butter and water in a medium bowl. Add the stuffing and stir lightly to coat.

3. Spoon into a 13×9×2-inch (3-quart) shallow baking dish. Top with the chicken.

4. Stir the soup and milk in a small bowl. Pour over the chicken. Top with the tomato. Sprinkle with the reserved stuffing mixture.

5. Bake at 400°F. for 30 minutes or until chicken is cooked through.   *Makes 4 servings*

Prep Time: 10 minutes
Cook Time: 30 minutes

Tempting Tetrazzini Casserole

1 can (26 ounces) CAMPBELL'S® Cream of Chicken Soup

1¼ cups milk

¾ cup grated Parmesan cheese

2 tablespoons dry sherry (optional)

1 teaspoon onion powder

3 cups cubed cooked chicken

1 jar (about 4½ ounces) sliced mushrooms, drained

4 cups hot cooked spaghetti

⅓ cup dry bread crumbs

2 tablespoons butter, melted

1. Mix soup, milk, cheese, sherry and onion powder. Add chicken, mushrooms and spaghetti and toss to coat. Spoon into 3-quart shallow baking dish.

2. Mix bread crumbs and butter and sprinkle on top.

3. Bake at 400°F. for 25 minutes or until hot.   *Makes 6 servings*

Prep Time: 20 minutes
Cook Time: 25 minutes

tip

For 3 cups cooked chicken, in 3-quart saucepan over medium heat, in 5 cups boiling water, cook about 1½ pounds skinless, boneless chicken breasts, cubed, 5 minutes or until chicken is no longer pink.

Alfredo Chicken & Asparagus Lasagna Roll-Ups

8 long lasagna noodles
1 cup diagonally sliced asparagus spears ($\frac{1}{2}$-inch pieces)
1 jar (16 ounces) alfredo pasta sauce, divided
2 cups (8 ounces) SARGENTO® BISTRO® Blends Shredded Italian Pasta Cheese, divided
$1\frac{1}{2}$ cups shredded or chopped cooked chicken
Basil sprigs or chopped fresh basil (optional)

COOK lasagna noodles according to package directions. Drain; rinse under cold water to stop the cooking. Arrange cooked noodles on work surface or on sheets of waxed paper. Cook asparagus in simmering water or in the microwave oven until crisp-tender; 1 to 2 minutes. Drain; rinse with cold water. Drain again; set aside.

MEANWHILE, spread $\frac{3}{4}$ cup of the pasta sauce in bottom of a 13×9-inch baking dish or pan. In a medium bowl, combine $1\frac{1}{4}$ cups of the cheese, $\frac{1}{2}$ cup of the pasta sauce, asparagus and chicken; mix well. Spoon heaping $\frac{1}{3}$ cup of the mixture down center of each lasagna noodle. Roll up; place seam-side down in dish. Spoon remaining sauce over rolls.

COVER dish with foil. Bake in preheated 375°F oven 30 minutes or until heated through. Uncover; sprinkle remaining $\frac{3}{4}$ cup cheese over rolls. Continue baking 5 minutes or until cheese is melted. Garnish with basil, if desired. *Makes 4 servings*

Prep Time: 25 minutes
Cook Time: 35 minutes

Cheesy Mexican Chicken

2 cups cooked chicken, diced
1 can ($10\frac{3}{4}$ ounces) reduced-sodium cream of chicken soup
$1\frac{1}{2}$ cups mild Cheddar cheese, shredded, divided*
1 cup milk
1 packet ($1\frac{1}{4}$ ounces) taco seasoning mix
1 cup MINUTE® White Rice, uncooked
2 cups tortilla chips, crushed

*Or use your favorite Mexican-style shredded cheese.

Preheat oven to 375°F. Mix chicken, soup, 1 cup cheese, milk and seasoning mix in medium saucepan. Bring to a boil. Remove from heat and stir in rice. Pour into 2-quart baking dish. Top with chips. Bake 15 minutes. Remove from oven and sprinkle with remaining $\frac{1}{2}$ cup cheese. *Makes 4 servings*

Quick Chicken Noodle Bake

1 can (10¾ ounces) CAMPBELL'S® Condensed Cream of Mushroom Soup
   (Regular or 98% Fat Free)
½ cup milk
1 cup cooked peas
2 cups cubed cooked chicken
2 cups medium egg noodles, cooked and drained
⅓ cup dry bread crumbs

1. Stir the soup, milk, peas, chicken and noodles in a 1½-quart casserole.

2. Bake at 400°F. for 15 minutes. Stir.

3. Top with bread crumbs. Bake for 15 minutes more or until hot.   *Makes 4 servings*

Prep Time: 10 minutes
Bake Time: 30 minutes

Homestyle Chicken & Rice Casserole

1 cup long grain white rice
1 can (14 ounces) chicken broth
¾ cup chopped onion
2 cups small broccoli florets
4 (2½ pounds) bone-in chicken breast halves
1 teaspoon paprika
1 teaspoon thyme leaves
1 teaspoon garlic salt
2 cups (8 ounces) SARGENTO® Fancy Shredded Mild Cheddar Cheese

COMBINE rice, broth, onion and broccoli in 11×7-inch baking pan. Place chicken over rice mixture. Combine paprika, thyme and garlic salt in small bowl; sprinkle over chicken.

COVER with foil; bake in preheated 375°F oven 40 minutes. Uncover; bake 15 minutes more or until liquid is absorbed, rice is tender and chicken is cooked through.

SPRINKLE chicken and rice with cheese. Bake 5 minutes more or until cheese is melted.

Makes 4 servings

Prep Time: 15 minutes
Cook Time: 60 minutes

Homestyle Chicken & Rice Casserole

Creamy Chicken Enchiladas

**1 can (10¾ ounces) CAMPBELL'S® Condensed Cream of Chicken Soup
   (Regular or 98% Fat Free)**
1 container (8 ounces) sour cream
1 cup picante sauce
2 teaspoons chili powder
2 cups chopped cooked chicken
1 cup shredded Monterey Jack cheese (4 ounces)
12 flour tortillas (8-inch), warmed
1 medium tomato, chopped (about 1 cup)
1 green onion, sliced (about 2 tablespoons)

1. Mix the soup, sour cream, picante sauce and chili powder in a small bowl.

2. Stir **1 cup** of the soup mixture, chicken and cheese in a medium bowl.

3. Spoon about ¼ **cup** of the chicken mixture down the center of each tortilla. Roll up the tortillas and place them seam-side down in 13×9-inch (3-quart) shallow baking dish. Pour the remaining soup mixture over the filled tortillas. **Cover**.

4. Bake at 350°F. for 40 minutes or until hot and bubbly. Top with the tomato and green onion.   *Makes 6 servings*

Prep Time: 20 minutes
Cook Time: 40 minutes

tip

Regardless of the cooking methods used, always cook chicken completely. Do not partially cook it and then store it to finish cooking later.

Buffalo Chicken Bake

$\frac{1}{3}$ **cup buffalo wing hot sauce**
$\frac{1}{4}$ **cup blue cheese dressing**
1 large egg, beaten
2 tablespoons melted butter
2 cans (15 ounces each) VEG•ALL® Original Mixed Vegetables, drained
3 cups cubed cooked chicken
3 cups cubed frozen hash brown potatoes, thawed
6 slices deli style Swiss cheese
$\frac{1}{2}$ **cup chopped celery leaves or chopped celery**

Preheat oven to 350°F.

In a large bowl, combine the first four ingredients. Stir until smooth. Add remaining ingredients except cheese and celery leaves. Toss to coat.

Transfer mixture to a greased 11×7-inch baking dish. Bake for 30 to 40 minutes.

Place cheese on top and bake for 10 more minutes. Sprinkle with celery leaves and serve.

Makes 4 to 6 servings

Prep Time: 15 minutes

No-Fuss Crispy Chicken Dinner

6 boneless skinless chicken breasts, cut into $1\frac{1}{2}$-inch strips (about $1\frac{1}{2}$ pounds)
2 packets extra-crispy seasoned coating mix
1 can ($10\frac{3}{4}$ ounces) condensed cream of chicken soup
1 soup can ($1\frac{1}{3}$ cups) water
2 cups MINUTE® White Rice, uncooked
1 package (16 ounces) frozen mixed vegetables

Preheat oven to 400°F. Moisten chicken with water. Shake off excess. Shake 3 or 4 strips at a time with coating mix. Discard any remaining coating mix.

Mix soup, water, rice and vegetables in 13×9-inch baking pan. Top with chicken strips.

Bake 45 minutes or until chicken is cooked through.

Makes 6 servings

Variation: Add 1 can (about 3 ounces) French fried onion rings, crushed, to the coating mix.

sandwiches & salads

Cheesy Chicken Ranch Sandwiches

6 small boneless, skinless chicken breast halves (1½ pounds)
⅔ cup KRAFT® Ranch Dressing, divided
6 ounces VELVEETA® Pasteurized Prepared Cheese Product, sliced
6 French bread rolls, split
6 large lettuce leaves

Preheat broiler. Spray rack of broiler pan with cooking spray; top with chicken. Brush with ⅓ cup of the dressing.

Broil, 3 to 4 inches from heat, 5 to 6 minutes on each side or until chicken is cooked through (165°F). Top with VELVEETA.® Broil an additional 2 minutes or until VELVEETA® is melted.

Spread cut sides of rolls evenly with remaining ⅓ cup dressing; fill with lettuce and chicken.

Makes 6 servings, 1 sandwich each.

Prep Time: 5 minutes
Total Time: 19 minutes

Serving Suggestion: Serve with your favorite fresh fruit.

Keeping It Safe: Use a visual test to ensure boneless chicken breasts are thoroughly cooked. Cut small slit in thickest part of chicken breast. If meat is totally white with no pink color, it is safe to eat.

Storage Know-How: Seal chicken in freezer-safe resealable plastic bag. Uncooked chicken can be kept frozen for up to 6 months; cooked chicken for up to 3 months.

Greek-Style Chicken and Bread Salad

2 slices stale whole wheat bread
1 clove garlic, halved
1 cup diced cooked chicken breast, chilled
1 cup halved cherry or grape tomatoes
1 small cucumber, peeled and diced
¼ cup thinly sliced green onions or ¼ cup thinly sliced red onion
4 teaspoons lemon juice
2½ tablespoons chicken broth
½ teaspoon olive oil
¼ teaspoon dried oregano
⅛ teaspoon black pepper
⅛ teaspoon salt (optional)

1. Rub each bread slice with garlic. Toast or grill bread until lightly browned and crisp. Tear into bite-size pieces. Combine bread, chicken, tomatoes, cucumber and green onions in large bowl; toss gently.

2. Whisk together lemon juice, broth, oil, oregano and pepper in small bowl. Pour over salad; toss gently. Season with salt, if desired. *Makes 2 servings*

Chicken Tuscan Sandwiches

½ cup HELLMANN'S® or BEST FOODS® Light Mayonnaise*
8 slices crusty Tuscan bread, toasted if desired
    Green leaf or romaine lettuce
1 pound sliced cooked chicken
    Sliced yellow and/or red beefsteak tomatoes
    Sliced Parmigiano-Reggiano or Asiago cheese
    Sliced red onion (optional)

Also terrific with HELLMANN'S® or BEST FOODS® Mayonnaise Dressing with Extra Virgin Olive Oil or Canola Cholesterol Free Mayonnaise.

Spread HELLMANN'S® or BEST FOODS® Light Mayonnaise on bread, then layer with lettuce, chicken, tomatoes, cheese and onion. *Makes 4 servings*

Prep Time: 10 minutes

Tip: Perk up the flavor of any sandwich the easy way. For a simple but delicious sandwich, marinate boneless skinless chicken breasts in WISH-BONE® Italian Dressing, broil or grill, and serve on a roll with lettuce, tomato and HELLMANN'S® or BEST FOODS® Real Mayonnaise.

Greek-Style Chicken and Bread Salad

Fiesta Chicken Sandwich

        2 tablespoons olive oil
        1 small onion, sliced
        1 medium red bell pepper, sliced
       12 ounces chicken tenders, cut in half lengthwise and crosswise
        1 cup guacamole
       12 slices (1 ounce each) pepper jack cheese
        2 packages (10 ounces each) 8-inch mini pizza crusts

1. Heat oil in large nonstick skillet over medium-high heat. Add onion and bell pepper; cook and stir 3 to 4 minutes or until crisp-tender. Remove vegetables with slotted spoon; set aside. Add chicken to skillet; cook and stir 4 minutes or until chicken is cooked through. Remove from skillet; wipe with paper towel.

2. Layer guacamole, chicken, vegetables and cheese evenly on one pizza crust; top with remaining pizza crust. Brush sandwich lightly with oil.

3. Heat same skillet over medium heat. Add sandwich; cook 4 to 5 minutes per side or until cheese melts and sandwich is golden brown. *Makes 4 servings*

Spinach, Chicken & Penne Toss

        1 package (5 ounces) DOLE® Baby Spinach with Tender Reds, Baby Arugula with
            Baby Spinach or other DOLE® Salad variety
        2 cups cooked penne pasta
    1½ cups shredded cooked deli-roasted chicken or deli-sliced chicken, cut into
            bite-size strips
       ⅔ cup slivered drained oil-packed sun-dried tomatoes
       ⅓ cup toasted pine nuts or slivered almonds
       ½ cup shredded Parmesan cheese
       ½ cup bottled red wine vinaigrette or balsamic vinegar dressing

• Place salad blend and all remaining ingredients except dressing in a large salad bowl.

• Toss ingredients well with salad dressing; serve immediately. *Makes 4 servings*

Prep Time: 15 minutes

Warm Gingered Chicken Salad
with Crispy Greens

½ cup HELLMANN'S® or BEST FOODS® Light Mayonnaise

2 teaspoons rice wine vinegar or white wine vinegar

1 teaspoon soy sauce

1 teaspoon honey

¼ teaspoon ground ginger

  Salt

1 tablespoon orange juice

4 boneless, skinless chicken breast halves (about 1¼ pounds)

6 cups torn romaine lettuce leaves

1 small bunch watercress (optional)

4 ounces snow peas (optional)

2 oranges, peeled and sectioned *or* 1 can (11 ounces) mandarin oranges, drained (optional)

1. Combine HELLMANN'S® or BEST FOODS® Light Mayonnaise, vinegar, soy sauce, honey, ginger and salt in small bowl. Reserve ¼ cup mayonnaise mixture for grilling. Stir orange juice into remaining mayonnaise mixture; reserve for greens.

2. Grill or broil chicken, brushing with reserved ¼ cup mayonnaise mixture, 12 minutes or until chicken is thoroughly cooked, turning once.

3. Toss lettuce and watercress, if desired, with reserved orange juice mixture in large bowl. To serve, arrange sliced chicken over greens, then top with snow peas and oranges, if desired.

Makes 4 servings

Prep Time: 20 minutes
Cook Time: 12 minutes

Variation: Also terrific with HELLMANN'S® or BEST FOODS® Low Fat Mayonnaise Dressing or HELLMANN'S® or BEST FOODS® Canola Cholesterol Free Mayonnaise.

California Chicken Ciabatta

**1 cup DOLE® Baby Romaine Blend or other DOLE® Salad variety,
   roughly chopped**
1 cup shredded cooked chicken
2 tablespoons slivered almonds
2 tablespoons dried cranberries
¼ cup mayonnaise
2 teaspoons Dijon-style mustard
⅛ teaspoon salt
⅛ teaspoon pepper
2 to 3 ciabatta or kaiser rolls
2 to 3 slices provolone cheese

• Combine chopped romaine, chicken, almonds and cranberries in large bowl.

• Stir together mayonnaise, mustard, salt and pepper. Pour over chicken mixture; toss to evenly coat.

• Slice rolls in half crosswise. Place provolone cheese on bottom halves of rolls. Evenly divide chicken mixture over cheese and top with top halves of rolls.   *Makes 2 to 3 servings*

Prep Time: 15 minutes

Chicken Caesar Salad

¼ cup plus 1 tablespoon Caesar salad dressing, divided
6 ounces chicken tenders, cut in half lengthwise and crosswise
    Black pepper
4 cups (about 5 ounces) prepared Italian salad mix (romaine and radicchio)
½ cup croutons, divided
2 tablespoons grated Parmesan cheese

1. Heat 1 tablespoon salad dressing in large nonstick skillet. Add chicken; cook and stir over medium heat 3 to 4 minutes or until chicken is cooked through. Remove chicken from skillet. Season with pepper; let cool.

2. Combine salad mix, ¼ cup croutons, remaining ¼ cup salad dressing and Parmesan cheese in serving bowl; toss to coat. Top with chicken and remaining ¼ cup croutons.

Makes 2 servings

Prep and Cook Time: 20 minutes

tip

Radicchio is a red-leafed variety of chicory, resembling a very small head of red cabbage. Young radicchio is green and turns red when the weather becomes cool. Radicchio has a sharp, slightly bitter flavor similar to Belgian endive.

Chicken Caesar Salad

Cobb Salad

1 package (10 ounces) torn mixed salad greens *or* 8 cups torn romaine lettuce
6 ounces cooked chicken breast, cut into bite-size pieces
1 tomato, seeded and chopped
2 hard-cooked eggs, cut into bite-size pieces
4 slices bacon, crisp-cooked and crumbled
1 ripe avocado, peeled and diced
1 large carrot, shredded
2 ounces blue cheese, crumbled
   Blue cheese dressing (optional)

1. Place salad greens in serving bowl. Arrange chicken, tomato, eggs, bacon, avocado, carrot and cheese on top of lettuce in rows.

2. Serve with dressing, if desired.   *Makes 4 servings*

Chicken Niçoise

⅓ cup HELLMANN'S® or BEST FOODS® Mayonnaise Dressing with
      Extra Virgin Olive Oil
⅓ cup WISH-BONE® Italian Dressing
1 pound boneless, skinless chicken breast halves
8 cups mixed salad greens
8 ounces green beans, halved, blanched and cooled
8 ounces new potatoes, quartered, cooked and cooled
¼ small red onion, thinly sliced
¼ cup sliced niçoise or oil-cured olives
1 cup cherry tomatoes, halved
2 hard-cooked eggs, sliced

1. In small bowl, blend HELLMANN'S® or BEST FOODS® Mayonnaise Dressing with Extra Virgin Olive Oil with Italian Dressing. Reserve 2 tablespoons; set aside.

2. On broiler pan, arrange chicken. Broil chicken, turning once and brushing with reserved mayonnaise mixture, 12 minutes or until chicken is thoroughly cooked. Cool; cut into cubes.

3. On large serving platter, arrange greens, then top with chicken, green beans, potatoes, onion, olives, tomatoes and eggs. Just before serving, toss with dressing.   *Makes 6 servings*

Prep Time: 30 minutes
Cook Time: 12 minutes

Mile-High Chicken Sandwich

1 tablespoon HELLMANN'S® or BEST FOODS® Real Mayonnaise
1 ciabatta roll, split
1 cooked chicken breast (about 3 ounces)
1 slice bacon, crisp-cooked
2 slices tomato
1 ounce sliced Cheddar cheese
Green leaf lettuce

Spread HELLMANN'S® or BEST FOODS® Real Mayonnaise evenly on roll, then top with chicken, bacon, tomato, cheese and lettuce.   *Makes 1 serving*

Prep Time: 10 minutes

Tip: Toss WISH-BONE® Italian Dressing with an assortment of beans to make a quick side salad.

Honey-Mustard Chicken Salad

4 ounces canned white chicken, rinsed and drained
½ cup sliced, seedless red grapes
¼ cup chopped water chestnuts
2 tablespoons honey-mustard salad dressing
¼ teaspoon grated lemon peel
1 teaspoon pine nuts
1 cup fresh spinach, washed, dried, stems removed
⅛ teaspoon black pepper

1. Toss chicken, grapes, water chestnuts, salad dressing and lemon peel in small bowl until well coated. Let stand 5 minutes for dressing to absorb.

2. Toast pine nuts in small nonstick skillet 2 minutes, shaking pan constantly.

3. Arrange spinach on plate; place salad on top of spinach. Sprinkle pine nuts on top; season with pepper.   *Makes 1 serving*

Mile-High Chicken Sandwich

Hot and Sweet Chicken Salad

1 medium jalapeño pepper,* seeded and minced
2 tablespoons apricot jam
2 tablespoons white wine vinegar
1 tablespoon vegetable oil
2 cups diced cooked chicken breast
1 stalk celery, thinly sliced, *or* ¼ cup roasted and salted almonds

*Jalapeño peppers can sting and irritate the skin, so wear rubber gloves when handling peppers and do not touch your eyes.

1. Combine jalapeño, jam, vinegar and oil in small bowl. Stir well. Place chicken in salad bowl. Pour dressing over chicken.

2. Just before serving, sprinkle with celery. Toss gently.   *Makes 4 servings*

Chopped Succotash Salad

8 cups chopped romaine lettuce leaves
1 pound cut-up cooked chicken
1 box (10 ounces) frozen lima beans, cooked, drained and rinsed with cold water
2 ears corn on the cob, kernels removed (about 2 cups) *or* 2 cups frozen corn kernels, thawed
1 large red bell pepper, chopped
½ cup chopped red onion
2 slices bacon, crisp-cooked and crumbled
60 sprays WISH-BONE® SALAD SPRITZERS® Ranch Dressing

On large shallow serving platter, arrange lettuce. Evenly top with remaining ingredients, arranging in rows. Just before serving, spritz with WISH-BONE® SALAD SPRITZERS® Ranch Dressing.   *Makes 6 servings*

Prep Time: 20 minutes

Variation: Try substituting your favorite vegetables!

Open-Face Chicken Sandwiches with Roasted Pepper Mayo

4 boneless skinless chicken breasts (about 4 ounces each)

1 teaspoon garlic salt

1 teaspoon dried thyme

¼ teaspoon black pepper

1 teaspoon olive oil or butter

¼ cup mayonnaise

1 jar (2 ounces) diced pimiento, drained *or* 3 tablespoons chopped roasted red bell pepper

4 slices multi-grain, rye or sourdough bread, lightly toasted

1 cup packed baby spinach or watercress sprigs

1. Place chicken between two sheets waxed paper or plastic wrap; pound to ⅓-inch thickness. Combine garlic salt, thyme and pepper in small bowl; sprinkle evenly over both sides of chicken.

2. Heat oil in large nonstick skillet over medium heat. Add chicken; cook 4 to 5 minutes per side or until no longer pink in center.

3. Meanwhile, combine mayonnaise and pimiento in small bowl until blended. Spread about 1½ teaspoons mayonnaise mixture on each toast slice. Place ¼ cup watercress on each toast slice. Top each with chicken breast half and 1½ teaspoons mayonnaise mixture.

Makes 4 servings

hot off the grill

Grilled Chicken with Southern Barbecue Sauce

Nonstick cooking spray
$^1/_2$ **cup chopped onion (about 1 small)**
4 **cloves garlic, minced**
1 **can (16 ounces) tomato sauce**
$^3/_4$ **cup water**
3 **tablespoons packed light brown sugar**
3 **tablespoons chili sauce**
2 **teaspoons** *each* **chili powder, dried thyme and Worcestershire sauce**
$^3/_4$ **teaspoon ground red pepper**
$^1/_2$ **teaspoon ground cinnamon**
$^1/_2$ **teaspoon black pepper**
6 **skinless bone-in chicken breasts (2$^1/_4$ pounds)**

1. Spray medium nonstick skillet with cooking spray; heat over medium heat. Add onion and garlic; cook and stir about 5 minutes or until tender.

2. Stir in tomato sauce, water, brown sugar, chili sauce, chili powder, thyme, Worcestershire, red pepper, cinnamon and black pepper; bring to a boil. Reduce heat to low and simmer uncovered, 30 minutes or until mixture is reduced to about $1^1/_2$ cups. Reserve $^3/_4$ cup sauce for basting. Meanwhile, prepare grill for indirect cooking.

3. Grill chicken covered, over medium heat 40 to 45 minutes or until cooked through (165°F), turning chicken several times and basting occasionally with reserved sauce.

4. Heat remaining sauce in same skillet over medium heat; spoon over chicken.

Makes 6 servings

Ginger-Lime Chicken Thighs

⅓ **cup vegetable oil**
3 **tablespoons lime juice**
3 **tablespoons honey**
2 **teaspoons grated fresh ginger** *or* **1 teaspoon ground ginger**
¼ **to** ½ **teaspoon red pepper flakes**
6 **boneless skinless chicken thighs**

1. Combine oil, lime juice, honey, ginger and pepper flakes in small bowl. Place chicken in large resealable food storage bag. Add ½ cup marinade. Seal bag; turn to coat. Marinate in refrigerator 30 to 60 minutes, turning occasionally.

2. Prepare grill for direct cooking.

3. Remove chicken from marinade; discard marinade. Place chicken on grid over medium-high heat. Grill chicken 12 minutes or until chicken is cooked through, turning once. Brush with reserved marinade during last 5 minutes of cooking. *Makes 2 to 4 servings*

Apricot-Glazed Chicken

¾ **cup WISH-BONE® Italian Dressing***
2 **teaspoons ground ginger (optional)**
2½ **to 3 pounds chicken, cut into serving pieces or chicken leg quarters**
¼ **cup apricot or peach preserves**
*Also terrific with WISH-BONE® Robusto Italian Dressing.

Blend Wish-Bone Italian Dressing and ginger in large, shallow nonaluminum baking dish or plastic bag. Pour ½ cup marinade over chicken; turn to coat. Cover, or close bag, and marinate in refrigerator, turning occasionally, 3 to 24 hours. Refrigerate remaining marinade.

Remove chicken from marinade, discarding marinade. In small saucepan, bring refrigerated marinade to a boil and continue boiling 1 minute. Remove from heat and stir in preserves until melted; set aside.

Grill or broil chicken, turning once and brushing frequently with preserve mixture during last 5 minutes of cooking, until chicken is thoroughly cooked (165°F). *Makes 4 servings*

Rustic Texas-Que Pizza

2 cups shredded, cooked chicken (about 1 pound uncooked)
¼ cup *Frank's*® *RedHot*® Buffalo Wings Sauce
1 pound prepared pizza or bread dough (thawed, if frozen)
1 cup *Cattlemen's*® Award Winning Classic Barbecue Sauce
2 ripe plum tomatoes, diced
½ cup finely diced red onion
½ cup sliced black olives (2.25 ounce can)
2 cups shredded taco blend cheese
   Cilantro or green onions, minced (optional)

1. Toss chicken with Buffalo Wings Sauce; set aside. Divide dough in half. Gently stretch or roll each piece of dough into 13×9-inch rectangle on floured surface. Coat one side with vegetable cooking spray.

2. Cook dough, coated side down, on greased grill over medium-high heat for 5 minutes until browned and crisp on bottom. Using tongs, turn dough over. Spread each pizza crust with barbecue sauce and top with chicken mixture, tomatoes, onion, olives and cheese, dividing evenly.

3. Grill pizzas about 5 minutes longer until bottom is browned, crispy and cheese melts. Garnish with minced cilantro or green onions, if desired.   *Makes 8 servings*

Prep Time: 15 minutes
Cook Time: 10 minutes

Variation: Top pizza with different shredded cheeses, such as Cheddar or Jack, or with other vegetables, such as whole kernel corn, jalapeño or bell peppers.

Tip: For easier handling, allow pizza dough to rest 30 minutes in an oiled, covered bowl at room temperature.

Spicy Grilled Chicken

4 boneless skinless chicken breasts
2 tablespoons minced garlic
1 tablespoon salt
1 tablespoon red pepper flakes
2 teaspoons paprika
2 teaspoons black pepper

1. Prepare grill for direct cooking over medium-high heat. Lightly score each chicken breast 3 or 4 times with knife.

2. Combine garlic, salt, pepper flakes, paprika and black pepper in small shallow bowl. Coat both sides of chicken with garlic mixture.

3. Grill chicken 8 to 10 minutes or until chicken is no longer pink in center, turning once.

Makes 4 servings

Serving Suggestion: Excellent served with rice pilaf.

Chicken Parmesan Packets

4 sheets (18×12 inches each) REYNOLDS WRAP® Heavy Duty Aluminum Foil
4 boneless, skinless chicken breast halves (1 pound)
1 cup pasta or pizza sauce
2 medium zucchini, sliced *or* 2 cups broccoli florets
¼ cup grated Parmesan cheese
1 cup shredded mozzarella cheese

Preheat grill to medium-high. Center 1 chicken breast half on each sheet of Reynolds Wrap® Heavy Duty Aluminum Foil. Spoon pasta sauce over chicken. Top with zucchini. Sprinkle with Parmesan cheese.

Bring up foil sides. Double fold top and ends to seal packet, leaving room for heat circulation inside. Repeat to make 4 packets.

Grill 12 to 14 minutes in covered grill. Sprinkle with mozzarella cheese before serving.

Makes 4 servings

Prep Time: 5 minutes
Grill Time: 20 minutes

Spicy Grilled Chicken

Mesquite-Grilled Chicken Quarters

2 whole chickens (about 3½ pounds each), cut into quarters
2 tablespoons vegetable oil
1 small onion, chopped
1 clove garlic, minced
1 can (12 ounces) beer
½ cup tomato juice
½ cup ketchup
¼ cup Worcestershire sauce
2 tablespoons brown sugar
1 tablespoon lemon juice
2 teaspoons chili powder
1 teaspoon dry mustard
¼ teaspoon salt
¼ teaspoon black pepper

1. Preheat oven to 350°F. Place chickens in one large or two medium baking pans; cover tightly with foil. Bake 30 minutes. Remove from oven; uncover. Cool.

2. Heat oil in 2-quart saucepan over medium heat. Add onion and garlic; cook until onion is tender. Whisk beer, tomato juice, ketchup, Worcestershire, sugar, lemon juice, chili powder, dry mustard, salt and pepper into saucepan until well blended. Bring to a boil. Reduce heat and simmer, stirring occasionally, 20 minutes or until sauce is thickened slightly and is reduced to about 2 cups. Let cool.

3. Place chickens into two large resealable food storage bags. Dividing marinade equally, pour over chicken in each bag; seal bags. Refrigerate 8 hours or overnight.

4. Prepare grill for direct cooking. Remove chickens from marinade and drain well; reserve marinade. Hook wing tips back behind body joint on breast pieces of chicken. Grill leg and thigh quarters on hottest part of grill 4 to 6 inches above heat; grill breast pieces on cooler edges of grill. Cook, turning occasionally, 20 to 25 minutes or until cooked through (165°F).

5. Meanwhile, place marinade in small saucepan; bring to a boil over medium-high heat. Boil 2 minutes; remove from heat and cool. Brush chicken generously with marinade during last 10 minutes of cooking. *Makes 8 servings*

Grilled Chicken Tostadas

    1 pound boneless skinless chicken breast halves
    1 teaspoon ground cumin
  ¼ cup plus 2 tablespoons hot or mild salsa, divided
  ¼ cup fresh orange juice
    1 tablespoon vegetable oil, plus additional for green onions
    2 cloves garlic, minced
    8 green onions
    1 can (16 ounces) refried beans
    4 (10-inch) or 8 (6- to 7-inch) flour tortillas
    2 cups sliced romaine lettuce leaves
 1½ cups (6 ounces) shredded Monterey Jack cheese with jalapeño peppers
    1 ripe medium avocado, pitted and diced (optional)
    1 medium tomato, seeded and coarsely chopped
    Chopped fresh cilantro (optional)
    Sour cream

1. Place chicken in single layer in shallow glass dish; sprinkle with cumin. Combine ¼ cup salsa, orange juice, 1 tablespoon oil and garlic in small bowl; pour over chicken. Cover; marinate in refrigerator at least 2 hours or up to 8 hours, stirring mixture occasionally.

2. Prepare grill for direct cooking.

3. Drain chicken; reserve marinade. Brush green onions with additional oil. Place chicken and green onions on grid. Grill covered, over medium heat 5 minutes. Brush tops of chicken with half of reserved marinade; turn and brush with remaining marinade. Turn onions. Continue to grill covered, 5 minutes or until chicken is no longer pink in center and onions are tender.

4. Meanwhile, combine beans and remaining 2 tablespoons salsa in small saucepan; cook, stirring occasionally, over medium heat until heated through.

5. Place tortillas in single layer on grid. Grill uncovered, 1 to 2 minutes per side or until golden brown. (If tortillas puff up, pierce with tip of knife or flatten by pressing with spatula.)

6. Transfer chicken and onions to carving board. Slice chicken crosswise into ½-inch-wide strips. Cut green onions crosswise into 1-inch-long pieces. Spread tortillas with bean mixture; top with lettuce, chicken, onions, cheese, avocado, if desired, and tomato. Sprinkle with cilantro. Serve with sour cream. *Makes 4 servings*

Carolina-Style Barbecue Chicken

2 pounds boneless skinless chicken breasts
¾ cup packed light brown sugar, divided
¾ cup *French's®* Classic Yellow® Mustard
½ cup cider vinegar
¼ cup *Frank's® RedHot®* Original Cayenne Pepper Sauce
2 tablespoons vegetable oil
2 tablespoons *French's®* Worcestershire Sauce
½ teaspoon salt
¼ teaspoon black pepper

1. Place chicken in large resealable plastic food storage bag. Combine ½ cup brown sugar, mustard, vinegar, Frank's RedHot Sauce, oil, Worcestershire, salt and pepper in 4-cup measure; mix well. Pour 1 cup mustard mixture over chicken. Seal bag; marinate in refrigerator 1 hour or overnight.

2. Pour remaining mustard mixture into small saucepan. Stir in remaining ¼ cup brown sugar. Bring to a boil. Reduce heat; simmer 5 minutes or until sugar dissolves and mixture thickens slightly, stirring often. Reserve for serving sauce.

3. Place chicken on well-oiled grid, reserving marinade. Grill over high heat 10 to 15 minutes or until chicken is no longer pink in center, turning and basting once with marinade. *Do not baste during last 5 minutes of cooking.* Discard any remaining marinade. Serve chicken with reserved sauce.   *Makes 8 servings*

Prep Time: 15 minutes
Marinate Time: 1 hour
Cook Time: 10 minutes

Carolina-Style Barbecue Chicken and Herbed Corn on the Cob (page 288)

Thai Coffee Chicken Skewers

1¼ **pounds chicken tenders**
⅓ **cup soy sauce**
¼ **cup strong brewed coffee**
2 **tablespoons plus 2 teaspoons lime juice, divided**
4 **cloves garlic, minced, divided**
1 **teaspoon grated fresh ginger**
½ **teaspoon sriracha or hot chili sauce, divided**
8 **(12-inch) bamboo skewers**
¼ **cup hoisin sauce**
2 **tablespoons creamy peanut butter**
1 **tablespoon tomato paste**
1 **teaspoon sugar**
½ **cup water**
1 **tablespoon minced ginger**
4 **green onions, cut into 1-inch pieces**

1. Cut chicken crosswise into ½-inch-wide strips; place in large resealable food storage bag. Add soy sauce, coffee, 2 tablespoons lime juice, 2 cloves garlic, 1 teaspoon ginger and ¼ teaspoon sriracha. Seal bag and shake well to coat. Marinate chicken in refrigerator 1 to 2 hours.

2. Soak skewers in water 30 minutes. Prepare grill for direct cooking. Whisk hoisin sauce, peanut butter, tomato paste, sugar, water, remaining 2 cloves garlic, ¼ teaspoon sriracha sauce, 2 teaspoons lime juice and 1 tablespoon ginger in medium mixing bowl. Set aside.

3. Remove chicken from marinade. Thread chicken strips onto each skewer, alternating with green onions. Grill skewers over medium heat 6 to 8 minutes or until chicken is cooked through, turning halfway through grilling time. Serve with peanut sauce.   *Makes 8 skewers*

Sesame Hoisin Beer-Can Chicken

      1 can (12 ounces) beer, divided
  ½ cup hoisin sauce
      2 tablespoons honey
      1 tablespoon soy sauce
      1 teaspoon chili-garlic sauce
  ½ teaspoon dark sesame oil
      1 whole chicken (3½ to 4 pounds)

1. Prepare grill for indirect cooking. Combine 2 tablespoons beer, hoisin sauce, honey, soy sauce, chili-garlic sauce and sesame oil in small bowl. Gently loosen skin of chicken over breast meat, legs and thighs. Spoon half of hoisin mixture under skin into cavity. Pour off beer until can is two-thirds full. Hold chicken upright with opening of cavity pointing down. Insert beer can into cavity.

2. Stand chicken upright on can over drip pan. Spread legs slightly to help support chicken. Grill covered, 30 minutes over medium indirect heat. Brush chicken with remaining hoisin mixture. Grill covered, 45 to 60 minutes or until chicken is cooked through (165°F). Use metal tongs to transfer chicken to cutting board; let rest, standing up, 5 minutes. Carefully remove beer can and discard. Carve chicken and serve.   *Makes 8 to 10 servings*

Chicken and Fruit Kabobs

  1¾ cups honey
  ¾ cup lemon juice
  ½ cup Dijon mustard
  ⅓ cup chopped fresh ginger
      4 pounds boneless skinless chicken breasts, cut into 1-inch pieces
      6 fresh plums, pitted and quartered
      3 firm bananas, cut into chunks
      4 cups fresh pineapple chunks (about half of medium pineapple)

1. Prepare grill for direct cooking. Combine honey, lemon juice, mustard and ginger in small bowl; mix well. Thread chicken onto skewers, alternating with fruit; brush generously with honey mixture.

2. Grill 5 minutes on each side, brushing frequently with honey mixture. Grill 10 minutes more or until chicken is cooked through, turning and brushing frequently with remaining honey mixture.   *Makes 12 servings*

Sesame Hoisin Beer-Can Chicken

Barbecued Chicken with Chile-Orange Glaze

1 to 2 dried chiles de arbol*
1½ teaspoons grated orange peel
½ cup orange juice
2 tablespoons tequila
2 cloves garlic, minced
¼ teaspoon salt
¼ cup vegetable oil
1 broiler-fryer chicken, cut into quarters (about 3 pounds)
Orange slices (optional)
Cilantro sprigs (optional)

*For milder flavor, discard seeds from chile peppers. Chile peppers can sting and irritate the skin, so wear rubber gloves when handling peppers and do not touch your eyes.

1. Crush chiles into coarse flakes in mortar with pestle. Combine chiles, orange peel, orange juice, tequila, garlic and salt in small bowl. Gradually whisk in oil until marinade is thoroughly blended.

2. Arrange chicken in single layer in shallow glass baking dish. Pour marinade over chicken; turn to coat. Cover and marinate in refrigerator 2 to 3 hours, turning chicken and basting with marinade several times.

3. Prepare grill for direct cooking. Drain chicken, reserving marinade. Bring marinade to a boil in small saucepan over high heat; boil 2 minutes. Grill chicken covered, 6 to 8 inches from heat 15 minutes, brushing frequently with marinade. Turn chicken. Grill 15 minutes or until chicken is cooked through (165°F), brushing frequently with marinade. *Do not baste during last 5 minutes of grilling.* Discard remaining marinade. Garnish with orange slices and cilantro.

Makes 4 servings

soups & stews

Spicy Squash & Chicken Soup

1 tablespoon vegetable oil
1 small onion, finely chopped
1 stalk celery, finely chopped
2 cups cubed delicata or butternut squash (about 1 small)
2 cups chicken broth
1 can (about 14 ounces) diced tomatoes with chiles
1 cup chopped cooked chicken
¹⁄₂ teaspoon ground ginger
¹⁄₄ teaspoon salt
¹⁄₈ teaspoon ground cumin
¹⁄₈ teaspoon black pepper
2 teaspoons lime juice
Fresh parsley or cilantro sprigs (optional)

1. Heat oil in large saucepan over medium heat. Add onion and celery; cook and stir 5 minutes or just until tender. Stir in squash, broth, tomatoes, chicken, ginger, salt, cumin and pepper.

2. Cover; cook over low heat 30 minutes or until squash is tender. Stir in lime juice. Sprinkle with parsley.

Makes 4 servings

Chicken and Herb Stew

½ **cup all-purpose flour**

½ **teaspoon salt**

¼ **teaspoon black pepper**

¼ **teaspoon paprika**

4 **chicken drumsticks**

4 **chicken thighs**

2 **tablespoons olive oil**

12 **ounces new potatoes, quartered**

2 **medium carrots, quartered lengthwise and cut into 3-inch pieces**

1 **green bell pepper, cut into thin strips**

¾ **cup chopped onion**

2 **medium cloves garlic, minced**

1¾ **cups water**

¼ **cup dry white wine**

2 **chicken bouillon cubes**

1 **tablespoon chopped fresh oregano**

1 **teaspoon chopped fresh rosemary**

2 **tablespoons chopped fresh parsley (optional)**

1. Combine flour, salt, black pepper and paprika in shallow dish. Stir until well blended. Coat chicken pieces with flour mixture; shake off excess.

2. Heat oil in large skillet over medium-high heat; add chicken. Brown evenly on both sides, turning frequently, about 8 minutes. Remove from skillet; set aside.

3. Add potatoes, carrots, bell pepper, onion and garlic to skillet. Cook and stir 5 minutes or until vegetables are lightly browned. Add water, wine and bouillon. Cook and stir, scraping browned bits from bottom of skillet. Stir in oregano and rosemary.

4. Place chicken pieces on top of vegetable mixture, turning several times to coat. Cover tightly and simmer 45 to 50 minutes or until chicken is cooked through (165°F), turning occasionally. Garnish with parsley.

Makes 4 servings

Moroccan Chicken Soup

**4 cups SWANSON® Chicken Broth (Regular, Natural Goodness® or
    Certified Organic)**
3 cloves garlic, minced
2 tablespoons honey
2 teaspoons ground cumin
½ teaspoon ground cinnamon
1 can (about 14½ ounces) diced tomatoes, undrained
1 large green pepper, cut into 2-inch-long strips (about 2 cups)
1 medium onion, chopped (1 cup)
½ cup raisins
8 skinless, boneless chicken thighs (about 1 pound), cut up
    Hot cooked orzo (optional)

Slow Cooker Directions

1. Stir the broth, garlic, honey, cumin, cinnamon, tomatoes, green pepper, onion and raisins in a 3½- to 6-quart slow cooker. Add the chicken.

2. Cover and cook on LOW for 8 hours* or until the chicken is cooked through.

3. Divide the soup among **4** serving bowls. Place about ½ **cup** orzo centered on top of **each** of the serving bowls.   *Makes 8 servings*

*Or on HIGH for 4 hours.

Prep Time: 10 minutes
Cook Time: 8 hours

Chunky Chicken Stew

1 teaspoon olive oil
1 small onion, chopped
1 cup *each* thinly sliced carrots and chicken broth
1 can (about 14 ounces) diced tomatoes
1 cup diced cooked chicken breast
3 cups sliced kale or baby spinach

1. Heat oil in large saucepan over medium heat. Add onion; cook and stir 5 minutes. Stir in carrots and broth; bring to a boil. Reduce heat; simmer uncovered, 5 minutes.

2. Stir in tomatoes; simmer 5 minutes or until carrots are tender. Add chicken; cook and stir until heated through. Add kale; stir until wilted.   *Makes 2 servings*

Moroccan Chicken Soup

Chicken and Chile Pepper Stew

1 pound boneless skinless chicken thighs, cut into ½-inch pieces
1 pound small potatoes, sliced
1 cup chopped onion
2 poblano peppers,* seeded and diced
1 jalapeño pepper,* seeded and finely chopped
3 cloves garlic, minced
3 cups chicken broth
1 can (about 14 ounces) diced tomatoes
2 tablespoons chili powder
1 teaspoon dried oregano

*Poblano and jalapeño peppers can sting and irritate the skin, so wear rubber gloves when handling peppers and do not touch your eyes.

Slow Cooker Directions

1. Place chicken, potatoes, onion, poblanos, jalapeño and garlic in slow cooker.

2. Combine broth, tomatoes, chili powder and oregano in large bowl. Pour broth mixture over chicken mixture in slow cooker; mix well. Cover; cook on LOW 8 to 9 hours.

Makes 6 servings

Easy Chicken, Spinach and Wild Rice Soup

1 can (about 14 ounces) chicken broth
1¾ cups chopped carrots
2 cans (10¾ ounces each) condensed cream of chicken soup
2 cups cooked wild rice
1 teaspoon dried thyme
¼ teaspoon dried sage
¼ teaspoon black pepper
2 cups coarsely chopped baby spinach
1½ cups cooked chicken
½ cup milk or half-and-half

1. Bring broth to a boil in medium saucepan. Add carrots; cook 10 minutes.

2. Add soup, rice, thyme, sage and pepper to saucepan; bring to a boil. Stir in spinach, chicken and milk. Cook and stir about 2 minutes or until heated through.

Makes 6 to 7 servings

Chicken and Chile Pepper Stew

Chunky Chicken Vegetable Soup

1 teaspoon vegetable oil

½ pound boneless skinless chicken breasts, cut into ½-inch cubes

1 can (14½ ounces) chicken broth

2 cups water

2 cups assorted cut-up vegetables (sliced carrots, broccoli florets, chopped red bell pepper)*

1 packet Italian salad dressing and recipe mix

1 cup MINUTE® White Rice, uncooked

2 tablespoons fresh parsley, chopped

*Or substitute 1 package (10 ounces) frozen mixed vegetables, thawed.

Heat oil in large saucepan over medium-high heat. Add chicken; cook and stir until browned.

Add broth, water, vegetables and salad dressing mix. Bring to a boil. Reduce heat to low; cover. Simmer 5 minutes.

Stir in rice and parsley; cover. Remove from heat. Let stand 5 minutes.   *Makes 4 servings*

Acorn Squash Soup with Chicken and Red Pepper Meatballs

1 acorn squash (about ¾ pound)

½ pound ground chicken

1 red bell pepper, seeded and finely chopped

3 tablespoons liquid egg whites

1 teaspoon dried parsley

1 teaspoon ground coriander

¼ teaspoon ground cinnamon

½ teaspoon black pepper

3 cups vegetable broth

2 tablespoons sour cream (optional)

Ground red pepper (optional)

1. Pierce squash skin with fork. Place in microwaveable dish; microwave on HIGH 8 to 10 minutes or until tender. Cool 10 minutes.

2. Combine chicken, bell pepper, egg whites, parsley, coriander, cinnamon and black pepper in large bowl. Form 8 meatballs; place in microwaveable dish. Microwave on HIGH 5 minutes or until cooked through; set aside to cool.

3. Scoop seeds out of cooled squash. Scrape squash flesh from shell into large saucepan; mash with potato masher. Add broth and meatballs; cook over medium-high heat 12 minutes, stirring occasionally, adding more liquid, if needed.

4. Garnish each serving with 1 tablespoon sour cream and sprinkle with red pepper.

Makes 2 servings

Chicken 'n' Black-Eyed Pea Soup

2 tablespoons olive oil

2 large onions, diced (about 2 cups)

3 large carrots, diced (about 2 cups)

2 medium parsnips, diced (about 2 cups)

2 medium potatoes, peeled and diced (about 2 cups)

1 tablespoon chopped fresh sage

5 cups SWANSON® Chicken Broth (Regular, Natural Goodness® or Certified Organic)

¾ pound cooked chicken, shredded or sliced (about 2½ cups)

1 can (about 15 ounces) black-eyed peas, rinsed and drained

1. Heat the oil in a 6-quart saucepot over medium heat. Add the onions, carrots, parsnips, potatoes and sage. Cook for 5 minutes. Add the broth. Heat to a boil. Reduce the heat to medium-low and cook for 20 minutes or until the vegetables are very tender.

2. Stir in the chicken and black-eyed peas. Cook until the mixture is hot. Season to taste.

Makes 8 servings

Prep Time: 20 minutes
Cook Time: 35 minutes

Easy Substitution Tip: Substitute 1 teaspoon dried sage leaves, crushed, for the fresh sage.

Easy Cajun Chicken Stew

     2 tablespoons vegetable oil
     1 red bell pepper, diced
     1 stalk celery, sliced
     1 can (about 14 ounces) diced tomatoes with roasted garlic and onions
  1½ cups chicken broth
     1 package (about 10 ounces) refrigerated fully cooked chicken breast strips, cut into pieces
     1 pouch (about 9 ounces) New Orleans-style chicken-flavored ready-to-serve rice mix
     1 cup canned kidney beans, rinsed and drained
     ¼ teaspoon hot pepper sauce
     ¼ cup chopped green onions

1. Heat oil in large saucepan or Dutch oven over medium-high heat. Add bell pepper and celery; cook and stir 3 minutes. Add tomatoes and broth; bring to a boil.

2. Add chicken, rice mix, beans and pepper sauce. Reduce heat to low. Cover; cook 7 minutes. Stir in green onions. Remove from heat. Cover; let stand 2 to 3 minutes to thicken.

Makes 4 servings

tip

If canned diced tomatoes with garlic and onions are not available, substitute 1 can (about 14 ounces) diced tomatoes, ¼ cup chopped onion and 1 teaspoon minced garlic.

Easy Cajun Chicken Stew

Green Chile Chicken Soup with Tortilla Dumplings

8 ORTEGA® Taco Shells, broken
½ cup water
⅓ cup milk
2 onions, diced, divided
1 egg
½ teaspoon POLANER® Minced Garlic
1 tablespoon olive oil
4 cups reduced-sodium chicken broth
2 cups shredded cooked chicken
2 tablespoons ORTEGA® Roasted Chiles
¼ cup vegetable oil

Place taco shells, water, milk, 1 diced onion, egg and garlic in blender or food processor. Pulse several times to crush taco shells and blend ingredients. Pour into medium bowl; let stand 10 minutes to thicken.

Heat 1 tablespoon olive oil in saucepan over medium heat. Add remaining diced onion; cook and stir 4 minutes or until translucent. Stir in broth, chicken and chiles. Reduce heat to a simmer.

Heat ¼ cup vegetable oil in small skillet over medium heat. Form taco shell mixture into 1-inch balls. Drop into hot oil in batches. Cook dumplings about 3 minutes or until browned. Turn over and continue cooking 3 minutes longer or until browned. Remove dumplings; drain on paper towels. Add dumplings to soup just before serving. *Makes 4 to 6 servings*

Prep Time: 15 minutes
Start to Finish: 30 minutes

Serving Suggestion: For an even more authentic Mexican flavor, garnish the soup with fresh chopped cilantro and a squirt of lime juice.

Green Chile Chicken Soup with Tortilla Dumplings

West African Chicken Stew

½ cup **all-purpose flour**
2 teaspoons **pumpkin pie spice**
1 teaspoon **paprika**
½ teaspoon **cracked black pepper**
6 **bone-in chicken thighs**
6 **chicken drumsticks**
2 tablespoons **vegetable oil**
1 can (10¾ ounces) **CAMPBELL'S® Condensed French Onion Soup**
½ cup **water**
1 cup **raisins***
½ cup **orange juice**
1 teaspoon **grated orange peel**
2 tablespoons **chopped fresh parsley or cilantro leaves**
6 cups **hot cooked couscous**

*You can substitute chopped prunes or apricots for the raisins, if you like.

Slow Cooker Directions

1. Mix the flour, pumpkin pie spice, paprika and black pepper on a plate. Coat the chicken with the flour mixture.

2. Heat the oil in a 12-inch skillet over medium heat. Add the chicken and cook for 10 minutes or until it's well browned.

3. Stir the soup, water, raisins, orange juice and orange peel in a 6-quart slow cooker. Add the chicken and turn to coat.

4. Cover and cook on LOW for 7 to 8 hours** or until the chicken is cooked through.

5. Stir the parsley into the cooker. Serve with the couscous.   *Makes 6 servings*

**Or on HIGH for 4 to 5 hours.

Prep Time: 15 minutes
Cook Time: 7 to 8 hours

Thyme for Chicken Stew with Polenta Dumplings

4 tablespoons olive oil, divided
2 pounds boneless skinless chicken thighs
2 medium eggplants, chopped
6 onions, chopped
4 tomatoes, seeded and diced
1 cup chicken broth
⅓ cup pitted black olives, sliced
1 tablespoon chopped fresh thyme *or* 1 teaspoon dried thyme
1 tablespoon red wine vinegar
Polenta Dumplings (recipe follows)

1. Preheat oven to 350°F.

2. Heat 1 tablespoon oil in 4-quart Dutch oven over medium-high heat. Cook chicken in batches 4 to 5 minutes or until browned on all sides. Remove and set aside.

3. Heat remaining 3 tablespoons oil in same Dutch oven; add eggplants, onions and tomatoes. Reduce heat to medium; cook and stir 5 minutes. Return chicken to Dutch oven. Stir in broth, olives, thyme and vinegar; bring to a boil. Transfer to oven; bake 1 hour. Meanwhile, prepare Polenta Dumplings.

4. Remove stew from oven; top with rounded tablespoonfuls dumpling mixture. Bake uncovered, about 20 minutes or until dumplings are cooked through. *Makes 6 servings*

Polenta Dumplings

3½ cups chicken broth
1 cup polenta or yellow cornmeal
½ cup grated Parmesan cheese
¼ cup chopped fresh parsley
1 egg, beaten
2 tablespoons butter

1. Bring broth to a boil in medium saucepan over medium-high heat. Gradually whisk in polenta. Reduce heat to low; simmer, stirring, about 15 minutes or until thickened.

2. Remove saucepan from heat; stir in cheese, parsley, egg and butter. *Makes 6 servings*

Sweet and Sour Chicken

   3 cloves garlic, minced
   2 tablespoons *each* rice vinegar and soy sauce
 ½ teaspoon minced fresh ginger
 ¼ teaspoon red pepper flakes (optional)
   6 ounces boneless skinless chicken breasts
   1 teaspoon vegetable oil
   3 green onions, cut into 1-inch pieces
   1 green bell pepper, cut into 1-inch pieces
   1 tablespoon cornstarch
 ½ cup chicken broth
   2 tablespoons apricot fruit spread
   1 can (11 ounces) mandarin orange segments, drained
   2 cups hot cooked white rice

1. Combine garlic, vinegar, soy sauce, ginger and pepper flakes, if desired, in medium bowl. Cut chicken into ½-inch strips; toss with vinegar mixture. Marinate 20 minutes at room temperature.

2. Heat oil in large nonstick skillet or wok over medium heat. Drain chicken; reserve marinade. Add chicken to skillet; cook and stir 3 minutes. Stir in green onions and bell pepper.

3. Stir cornstarch into reserved marinade. Stir broth, fruit spread and marinade mixture into skillet. Cook and stir until chicken is cooked through and sauce boils 1 minute and thickens. Add orange segments; heat through. Serve over rice.   *Makes 4 servings*

Double-Quick Mozzarella Chicken

4 boneless skinless chicken breasts (about 1 pound)
Juice of 1 lemon
1 teaspoon ground cumin
¼ teaspoon salt
¾ cup (3 ounces) shredded mozzarella cheese
½ (10-ounce) can Mexican-style diced tomatoes with green chiles, drained
2 tablespoons chopped fresh cilantro (optional)

1. Preheat oven to 400°F. Line baking sheet with foil. Arrange chicken breasts about 2 inches apart. Drizzle lemon juice over chicken. Sprinkle with cumin and salt. Bake 20 minutes.

2. Sprinkle cheese evenly over chicken; bake 5 minutes or until chicken is no longer pink in center. Transfer to serving platter. Spoon about 3 tablespoons diced tomatoes over each chicken breast. Sprinkle with cilantro.

Makes 4 servings

tip

This dish is excellent served with no-yolk egg noodles and green beans.

Cilantro-Lime Chicken

1 lime
2 tablespoons vegetable oil
1 pound boneless skinless chicken breasts, cut into 1-inch pieces
1 or 2 small jalapeño peppers,* seeded and sliced
1 (1-inch) piece fresh ginger, peeled and thinly sliced
2 small onions, cut into wedges
2 tablespoons chopped fresh cilantro
2 tablespoons soy sauce
1 to 2 teaspoons sugar
Flour tortillas

*Jalapeño peppers can sting and irritate the skin, so wear rubber gloves when handling peppers and do not touch your eyes.

1. Remove 3 strips of peel from lime with vegetable peeler. Cut lime peel into very fine shreds. Juice lime; measure 2 tablespoons juice. Set aside.

2. Heat oil in large skillet or wok over medium-high heat. Add chicken, jalapeño and ginger; cook and stir 3 minutes or until chicken is cooked through. Reduce heat to medium.

3. Add onions; cook and stir 5 minutes.

4. Add lime peel, juice and cilantro; cook and stir 1 minute. Add soy sauce and sugar; cook and stir until heated through. Serve with tortillas. *Makes 4 servings*

Crunchy Pecan Chicken

4 boneless, skinless chicken breast halves
4 teaspoons honey mustard
⅓ cup finely chopped pecans
⅓ cup Italian seasoned bread crumbs
2 tablespoons butter or margarine, melted
¼ teaspoon salt

Arrange chicken in a single layer in a shallow baking pan. Brush top of each chicken piece with one teaspoon honey mustard. In a small bowl, mix together pecans, bread crumbs, butter and salt. Sprinkle nut mixture evenly over chicken. Bake in 400°F oven 30 minutes or until chicken is browned and fork-tender. *Makes 4 servings*

Favorite recipe from **Delmarva Poultry Industry, Inc.**

Cilantro-Lime Chicken

Oven-Fried Chicken

3 tablespoons all-purpose flour
½ teaspoon poultry seasoning
¼ teaspoon *each* garlic salt and black pepper
1½ cups cornflakes, crushed
1 tablespoon dried parsley
1 egg white
1 tablespoon water
4 boneless skinless chicken breasts (about 4 ounces each)
4 skinless chicken drumsticks (about 2½ ounces each)
Nonstick cooking spray

1. Preheat oven to 375°F.

2. Combine flour, poultry seasoning, garlic salt and pepper in large resealable food storage bag. Combine cornflakes and parsley in small bowl. Whisk egg white and water in another small bowl.

3. Add chicken to flour mixture 1 or 2 pieces at a time. Seal bag; shake until well coated. Remove chicken from bag, shaking off excess flour. Dip into egg white mixture, coating all sides. Roll in cornflake mixture. Place in shallow baking pan. Lightly spray chicken with cooking spray.

4. Bake chicken breasts 18 to 20 minutes or until no longer pink in center. Bake drumsticks about 25 minutes or until cooked through (165°F). *Makes 4 servings*

Ya Gotta Empanada

1 package (4.4 to 6.8 ounces) Spanish rice mix, prepared according
   to package directions
1 cup shredded cooked chicken
1 cup (4 ounces) shredded Cheddar cheese
½ cup sliced green onions
¼ cup chopped black olives
1 package (15 ounces) refrigerated pie crust

Combine rice, chicken, cheese, onions and olives in large bowl. Spoon half of rice mixture on half of each pie crust. Fold crust over filling. Seal and crimp edges. Place on baking sheet. Bake at 400°F 20 to 22 minutes or until golden brown. Cut each empanada in half. Serve immediately. *Makes 4 servings*

Favorite recipe from **USA Rice**

Oven-Fried Chicken

Rustic Dijon Chicken with Tomato Pesto

1 tablespoon olive oil

1 teaspoon minced garlic

4 boneless skinless chicken breast halves (1 pound)

1 can (14½ ounces) diced tomatoes or crushed tomatoes in purée, undrained

1 container (4 ounces) prepared pesto sauce

1⅓ cups *French's*® French Fried Onions, divided

2 tablespoons *French's*® Honey Dijon Mustard

Hot cooked noodles or pasta

1. Heat oil in 12-inch nonstick skillet over medium-high heat. Add garlic; sauté 30 seconds. Add chicken; sauté 5 minutes or until chicken is browned on both sides.

2. Add tomatoes with juice, pesto sauce, *1 cup* French Fried Onions and mustard. Reduce heat to medium-low. Simmer 5 minutes or until chicken is no longer pink in center and sauce thickens slightly.

3. To serve, arrange chicken over hot cooked noodles or pasta. Top with sauce and sprinkle with remaining onions. *Makes 4 servings*

Prep Time: 5 minutes
Cook Time: 10 minutes

Chicken with Spinach and Celery Hash

1 package (16 ounces) refrigerated precooked hash brown potatoes
1 package (8 ounces) celery, thinly sliced
3 teaspoons olive oil, divided
12 chicken tenders (about 1 pound)
½ teaspoon dried thyme
¼ teaspoon ground white pepper
2 packages (5 ounces each) baby spinach
¼ cup water

1. Combine potatoes and celery in medium bowl.

2. Heat 1½ teaspoons oil in large nonstick skillet over medium-high heat. Add potato mixture; cook about 10 minutes, stirring and turning occasionally until mixture begins to brown. Reduce heat; cook 10 minutes or until mixture is browned.

3. Meanwhile, heat remaining 1½ teaspoons oil in another large nonstick skillet over medium-high heat. Add chicken, thyme and pepper. Cook about 5 minutes or until cooked through, turning once. Remove from skillet; keep warm.

4. Add spinach and water to same skillet. Cover; cook about 3 minutes, stirring once.

5. To serve, divide spinach and hash brown mixture among 4 plates. Top with 3 chicken tenders.

Makes 4 servings

tip

Chicken tenders may have white edible tendons. They may become tough when cooked. To remove them, lay each chicken tender flat and hold down the larger end. While pulling on the tendon, slide a knife between it and the meat.

Chicken and Vegetables with Mustard Sauce

1 tablespoon sugar
2 teaspoons cornstarch
2 teaspoons dry mustard
3 tablespoons soy sauce
2 tablespoons water
2 tablespoons rice vinegar
2 tablespoons vegetable oil, divided
1 pound boneless skinless chicken breasts, cut into 1-inch pieces
2 cloves garlic, minced
1 red bell pepper, cut into thin slices
½ cup thinly sliced celery
1 small onion, cut into thin wedges
  Chinese egg noodles
  Fresh chives (optional)

1. Combine sugar, cornstarch and mustard in small bowl. Stir soy sauce, water and vinegar into cornstarch mixture until smooth; set aside.

2. Heat 1 tablespoon oil in large skillet or wok over medium heat. Add chicken and garlic; cook and stir 5 to 6 minutes or until chicken is cooked through. Remove chicken to large bowl.

3. Drizzle remaining oil into skillet and heat 30 seconds. Add pepper, celery and onion; cook and stir 3 minutes or until vegetables are crisp-tender.

4. Stir soy sauce mixture; add to skillet. Cook and stir 30 seconds or until sauce boils and thickens.

5. Return chicken and any accumulated juices to skillet; cook until heated through. Serve with noodles. Garnish with fresh chives. *Makes 4 servings*

Make-Ahead Dill Chicken in Foil

 8 chicken thighs, skinned
 1 teaspoon salt
½ teaspoon ground black pepper
½ cup butter or margarine, melted
 2 tablespoons lemon juice
 1 teaspoon dried dill weed
   Vegetable cooking spray
 3 green onions, thinly sliced
 1 cup thinly sliced carrots
 6 ounces Swiss cheese, cut into 8 slices

Sprinkle chicken thighs with salt and pepper. Combine butter, lemon juice and dill in small bowl. Cut four 12-inch squares of heavy-duty foil; coat each with cooking spray. Place 1 tablespoon dill-butter sauce on center of each foil square; place 2 chicken thighs on sauce. Divide onion and carrot slices evenly over chicken. Top each with additional 1 tablespoon sauce and 1 slice cheese. Fold foil into packets, sealing securely.* To serve, place packets in baking pan and bake at 400°F 35 to 40 minutes or until fork can be inserted into chicken with ease and juices run clear, not pink.   *Makes 4 servings*

*Chicken may be frozen for up to 9 months. Label, date and freeze chicken. To serve, place frozen foil packets in baking pan and bake at 400°F 1 hour or until fork can be inserted into chicken with ease and juices run clear, not pink.

Favorite recipe from **National Chicken Council**

Kung Pao Chicken

5 teaspoons dry sherry, divided

5 teaspoons soy sauce, divided

3½ teaspoons cornstarch, divided

¼ teaspoon salt

3 boneless skinless chicken breasts (about 1 pound), cut into bite-size pieces

2 tablespoons chicken broth

1 tablespoon red wine vinegar

1½ teaspoons sugar

3 tablespoons vegetable oil, divided

⅓ cup salted peanuts

6 to 8 small dried red chiles

1½ teaspoons minced fresh ginger

2 green onions, cut into 1½-inch pieces

1. For marinade, combine 2 teaspoons sherry, 2 teaspoons soy sauce, 2 teaspoons cornstarch and salt in large bowl; mix well. Add chicken; stir to coat. Let stand 30 minutes.

2. Combine remaining 3 teaspoons sherry, 3 teaspoons soy sauce, 1½ teaspoons cornstarch, chicken broth, vinegar and sugar in small bowl.

3. Heat 1 tablespoon oil in large skillet or wok over medium heat. Add peanuts; cook and stir until lightly toasted. Remove and set aside. Heat remaining 2 tablespoons oil in skillet over medium heat. Add chiles; cook and stir until chiles just begin to char, about 1 minute.

4. Increase heat to high. Add chicken mixture; cook and stir 2 minutes. Add ginger; cook and stir until chicken is cooked though, about 1 minute. Stir in peanuts and green onions. Stir cornstarch mixture; add to skillet. Cook and stir until sauce boils and thickens.

Makes 3 servings

Chicken-Pesto Pizza

½ **pound chicken tenders**
   Nonstick cooking spray
1 **medium onion, thinly sliced**
⅓ **cup prepared pesto**
3 **medium plum tomatoes, thinly sliced**
1 **(14-inch) prepared pizza crust**
1 **cup (4 ounces) shredded mozzarella cheese**

1. Preheat oven to 450°F. Cut chicken tenders into bite-size pieces. Coat medium nonstick skillet with cooking spray; cook and stir chicken over medium heat 2 minutes. Add onion and pesto; cook and stir about 3 minutes or until chicken is cooked through.

2. Arrange tomato slices and chicken mixture on pizza crust to within 1 inch of edge. Sprinkle with cheese. Bake 8 minutes or until pizza is hot and cheese is melted and bubbly.

Makes 6 servings

Prep and Cook Time: 22 minutes

Chicken and Ham Jambalaya

2 **tablespoons vegetable oil**
1 **pound boneless skinless chicken breasts, cut into 1-inch chunks**
1 **cup chopped onion**
¼ **cup diced green bell pepper**
1 **can (28 ounces) diced tomatoes seasoned with garlic, oregano and basil**
1 **slice (¼ inch thick) ham, cut into 2-inch strips**
1 **teaspoon salt**
½ **teaspoon sugar**
1 **bay leaf**
2 **cups cooked rice**

1. Heat oil in large skillet over medium-high heat. Add chicken, onion and pepper; cook and stir 8 minutes or until chicken is cooked through.

2. Add tomatoes, ham, salt, sugar and bay leaf; reduce heat to low and simmer 5 minutes.

3. Stir in rice; cover and simmer 10 minutes or until heated through. Remove and discard bay leaf.

Makes 4 to 6 servings

ultimate
burgers

Classic California Burgers

2 tablespoons *French's*® **Honey Dijon Mustard**
2 tablespoons mayonnaise
2 tablespoons sour cream
1 pound ground beef
2 tablespoons *French's*® **Worcestershire Sauce**
1⅓ cups *French's*® **Cheddar or Original French Fried Onions, divided**
½ teaspoon garlic salt
¼ teaspoon ground black pepper
4 hamburger rolls, split and toasted
½ small avocado, sliced
½ cup sprouts

1. Combine mustard, mayonnaise and sour cream; set aside.

2. Combine beef, Worcestershire, *⅔ cup* French Fried Onions and seasonings. Form into 4 patties. Grill over high heat until juices run clear (160°F internal temperature).

3. Place burgers on rolls. Top each with mustard sauce, avocado slices, sprouts and remaining onions, dividing evenly. Cover with top halves of rolls. *Makes 4 servings*

Prep Time: 10 minutes
Cook Time: 10 minutes

BBQ Cheese Burgers: Top each burger with 1 slice American cheese, 1 tablespoon barbecue sauce and 2 tablespoons French Fried Onions.

Pizza Burgers: Top each burger with pizza sauce, mozzarella cheese and French Fried Onions.

Curried Beef Burgers

 1 pound ground beef
 ¼ cup mango chutney, chopped
 ¼ cup grated apple
 1½ teaspoons curry powder
 ½ teaspoon salt
 ⅛ teaspoon black pepper
 1 large red onion, cut into ¼-inch slices
   Lettuce leaves
 4 Kaiser rolls or hamburger buns
 1 large tomato, sliced

1. Preheat grill. Combine beef, chutney, apple, curry powder, salt and pepper in medium bowl; mix lightly. Shape into 4 patties.

2. Grill covered, over medium heat 8 to 10 minutes (uncovered 13 to 15 minutes) or until cooked through (160°F), turning once. Grill onion 5 minutes or until lightly charred, turning once. Place lettuce on bottom halves of rolls. Top with burgers, tomatoes, onion and top halves of rolls.   *Makes 4 servings*

Bacon-Cheese Burgers with Orange Salsa

 2 large oranges, peeled and diced
 1 jalapeño pepper, seeded and finely chopped
 1 large shallot, finely chopped
 1 tablespoon minced fresh cilantro
 1 teaspoon *each* honey and cider vinegar
 ¼ teaspoon salt
 4 slices bacon
 1 pound ground beef
 ½ cup (2 ounces) shredded sharp Cheddar cheese

1. For orange salsa, combine oranges, jalapeño, shallot, cilantro, honey, vinegar and salt in medium bowl. Stir until well blended; set aside.

2. Cook bacon in large skillet until very crisp. Drain on paper towels; crumble or chop into small pieces. Discard all but 1 tablespoon bacon drippings from skillet.

3. Combine bacon, beef and cheese in large bowl; stir gently until just mixed. Shape into 4 patties. Cook in bacon drippings about 5 minutes per side or until cooked through (160°F). Serve with orange salsa.   *Makes 4 servings*

Curried Beef Burger

BBQ Burgers with Coleslaw

¼ cup light sour cream

1 teaspoon sugar

1 teaspoon apple cider vinegar

¼ teaspoon dry mustard

¼ teaspoon garlic powder

2 cups DOLE® Classic Cole Slaw

Salt and black pepper

Paprika

1¼ pounds ground beef

½ cup prepared barbecue sauce, divided

4 sesame seed hamburger buns, split

• Mix sour cream, sugar, vinegar, mustard and garlic. Toss with cole slaw blend; season with salt, pepper and paprika to taste.

• Mix meat with 2 tablespoons barbecue sauce; season with salt and pepper. Form meat into 4½-inch patties. Grill over medium-high heat, brushing frequently with barbecue sauce, 5 to 6 minutes on each side or until cooked to desired temperature. Toast the buns, cut side down, just before serving.

• Place patty on bottom half of each bun. Top with ½ cup coleslaw and other half of bun. Serve with roasted potato wedges. *Makes 4 servings*

Prep Time: 35 minutes

Pineapple Variation: Add ½ cup diced fresh DOLE® pineapple.

Beef Burgers with Corn Salsa

½ **cup frozen corn**
½ **cup peeled, seeded, chopped tomato**
1 **can (about 4 ounces) diced green chiles, divided**
1 **tablespoon chopped fresh cilantro** *or* **1 teaspoon dried cilantro**
1 **tablespoon vinegar**
1 **teaspoon olive oil**
¼ **cup fine dry bread crumbs**
3 **tablespoons milk**
¼ **teaspoon garlic powder**
12 **ounces ground beef**
   Lettuce leaves

1. Prepare corn according to package directions; drain. Combine corn, tomato, 2 tablespoons chiles, cilantro, vinegar and oil in small bowl. Cover and refrigerate.

2. Preheat broiler. Combine bread crumbs, remaining chiles, milk and garlic powder in medium bowl. Add beef; mix lightly. Shape mixture into 4 patties. Place on broiler pan.

3. Broil patties 4 inches from heat 6 to 8 minutes. Turn and broil 6 to 8 minutes or until cooked through (160°F). Serve on lettuce leaves; spoon salsa over burgers.   *Makes 4 servings*

Pizza Burgers

1 **pound ground beef**
1 **cup (4 ounces) shredded mozzarella cheese**
1 **tablespoon minced onion**
1 **tablespoon chopped fresh basil** *or* **1 teaspoon dried basil**
1½ **teaspoons chopped fresh oregano** *or* ½ **teaspoon dried oregano**
½ **teaspoon salt**
   Dash black pepper
   Prepared pizza sauce, warmed
4 **English muffins**

1. Preheat grill. Combine beef, cheese, onion, basil, oregano, salt and pepper in medium bowl; mix lightly. Shape into 4 patties.

2. Grill covered, over medium heat 8 to 10 minutes (uncovered 13 to 15 minutes) or until cooked through (160°F), turning once. Top with pizza sauce. Serve on English muffins.

Makes 4 servings

Beef Burgers with Corn Salsa

Velveeta® Wow! Burger

What You Need

1½ **pounds extra lean ground beef**

6 **ounces VELVEETA® 2% Milk Pasteurized Prepared Cheese Product,
cut into 6 slices**

6 **whole wheat hamburger buns, toasted**

1 **can (10 ounces) diced tomatoes & green chilies, drained**

Make It

1. HEAT grill to medium heat. Shape meat into 6 (¾-inch-thick) patties.

2. GRILL 7 to 9 minutes on each side or until done (160°F). Top with VELVEETA®; grill 1 to 2 minutes or until melted.

3. PLACE cheeseburgers on bottom halves of buns; cover with tomatoes and tops of buns.

Makes 6 servings

Prep Time: 10 minutes
Total Time: 30 minutes

Serving Suggestion: Serve with fresh fruit and assorted cut-up fresh vegetables.

How to Use Your Stove: Cook patties in skillet on medium heat 4 to 6 minutes on each side or until done (160°F). Top with VELVEETA®; cover with lid. Cook 1 to 2 minutes or until VELVEETA® is melted. Continue as directed.

Spicy Burrito Burgers

6 **tablespoons mild salsa, divided**

1 **can (about 4 ounces) diced green chiles, divided**

¼ **cup sour cream**

Dash hot pepper sauce

1 **pound ground beef**

4 **(8-inch) flour tortillas**

1 **cup shredded lettuce**

½ **cup (2 ounces) taco-flavored shredded Cheddar cheese**

1. Combine 2 tablespoons salsa, 2 tablespoons chiles, sour cream and pepper sauce in small bowl; set aside.

2. Combine beef, remaining 4 tablespoons salsa and remaining chiles in large bowl; mix well. Shape into 4 oval patties.

3. Grill over medium heat 8 to 10 minutes or until cooked through (160°F), turning once.

4. Place burger in center of each tortilla. Top evenly with lettuce, cheese and sour cream mixture. Bring edges of tortillas together over top of burgers; secure with toothpicks if necessary. Remove toothpicks before serving. *Makes 4 servings*

Southwest Pesto Burgers

½ **cup fresh cilantro, stemmed**

1½ **teaspoons chopped jalapeño pepper *or* 1 tablespoon sliced jalapeño pepper,* drained**

1 **clove garlic**

¾ **teaspoon salt, divided**

¼ **cup vegetable oil**

2 **tablespoons mayonnaise**

1¼ **pounds ground beef**

4 **slices pepper jack cheese**

4 **Kaiser rolls, split**

1 **ripe avocado, sliced**

Salsa

*Jalapeño peppers can sting and irritate the skin, so wear rubber gloves when handling peppers and do not touch your eyes.

1. Combine cilantro, jalapeño, garlic and ¼ teaspoon salt in food processor; process until garlic is minced. Slowly add oil through feed tube; process until thick paste forms. Cover and refrigerate until serving time.

2. Prepare grill for direct cooking. Combine mayonnaise and 1 tablespoon pesto in small bowl; mix well.

3. Combine beef, remaining ¼ cup pesto and ½ teaspoon salt in large bowl; mix lightly. Shape into 4 patties. Grill uncovered, over medium heat 8 to 10 minutes (uncovered 13 to 15 minutes) or until cooked through (160°F), turning occasionally. Top burgers with cheese during last minute of grilling.

4. Place patties on bottom halves of rolls. Top with mayonnaise mixture, avocado and salsa. Cover with top halves of rolls. *Makes 4 servings*

Ranchero Onion Burgers

   1 pound ground beef
   ½ cup salsa
   ½ cup (2 ounces) shredded Monterey Jack cheese
   1⅓ cups *French's*® Cheddar or Original French Fried Onions, divided
   ½ teaspoon garlic powder
   ¼ teaspoon ground black pepper
   4 hamburger rolls

Combine beef, salsa, cheese, ⅔ *cup* French Fried Onions, garlic powder and pepper in large bowl. Shape into 4 patties.

Place patties on oiled grid. Grill* over medium coals 10 minutes or until no longer pink in center, turning once. Serve on rolls. Garnish with additional salsa, if desired. Top with remaining ⅔ *cup* onions.   *Makes 4 servings*

*Or broil 6 inches from heat.

Prep Time: 10 minutes
Cook Time: 10 minutes

Serving Suggestion: For Salsa Olé, combine 1½ cups prepared salsa with ¼ cup *Frank's® Redhot®* Hot Sauce.

tip

For extra-crispy warm onion flavor, heat French Fried Onions in the microwave for 1 minute. Or place in foil pan and heat on the grill 2 minutes.

Ranchero Onion Burger

Blue Cheese Burgers

1¼ **pounds ground beef**
1 **tablespoon finely chopped onion**
1½ **teaspoons chopped fresh thyme** *or* ½ **teaspoon dried thyme**
¾ **teaspoon salt**
  Dash black pepper
4 **ounces blue cheese, crumbled**
  Dijon mustard (optional)
4 **whole wheat hamburger buns**
  Lettuce leaves
  Tomato slices

1. Prepare grill for direct cooking.

2. Combine beef, onion, thyme, salt and pepper in medium bowl; mix lightly. Shape into 8 patties.

3. Place cheese in center of 4 patties to within ½ inch of outer edge; top with remaining patties. Press edges together to seal.

4. Grill covered, over medium heat 8 to 10 minutes (uncovered 13 to 15 minutes) or until cooked through (160°F), turning once. Spread mustard on bottom halves of buns, if desired. Top with lettuce, tomato, burgers and top halves of buns. *Makes 4 servings*

Tempting Taco Burgers

1 **envelope LIPTON® RECIPE SECRETS® Onion Mushroom Soup Mix***
1 **pound ground beef**
½ **cup chopped tomato**
¼ **cup finely chopped green bell pepper**
1 **teaspoon chili powder**
¼ **cup water**

Also terrific with LIPTON® RECIPE SECRETS® Onion or Beefy Onion Soup Mix.

1. In large bowl, combine all ingredients; shape into 4 patties.

2. Grill or broil until no longer pink in center (160°F). Serve, if desired, on hamburger buns and top with shredded lettuce and Cheddar cheese. *Makes 4 servings*

Blue Cheese Burger

Brie Burgers with Sun-Dried Tomato and Artichoke Spread

1 cup canned quartered artichokes, drained and chopped
$\frac{1}{2}$ cup sun-dried tomatoes packed in oil, drained and chopped, divided
2 tablespoons mayonnaise
1 tablespoon plus 1 teaspoon minced garlic, divided
1 teaspoon black pepper, divided
$\frac{1}{2}$ teaspoon salt, divided
$1\frac{1}{2}$ pounds ground beef
$\frac{1}{4}$ cup chopped shallots
$\frac{1}{4}$ pound Brie, sliced
2 tablespoons butter, softened
4 egg or Kaiser rolls, split
Heirloom tomato slices
Arugula or lettuce leaves

1. Prepare grill for direct cooking.

2. Combine artichokes, $\frac{1}{4}$ cup tomatoes, mayonnaise, 1 teaspoon garlic, $\frac{1}{2}$ teaspoon pepper and $\frac{1}{4}$ teaspoon salt in small bowl; mix well.

3. Combine beef, shallots, remaining $\frac{1}{4}$ cup tomatoes, 1 tablespoon garlic, $\frac{1}{2}$ teaspoon pepper and $\frac{1}{4}$ teaspoon salt in large bowl; mix lightly. Shape into 4 patties.

4. Grill covered, 8 to 10 minutes (uncovered 13 to 15 minutes) or until cooked through (160°F), turning occasionally. Top each burger with cheese during last 2 minutes of grilling.

5. Spread butter on cut surfaces of rolls; toast or grill until lightly browned. Spread artichoke mixture over bottom halves of rolls. Top with tomato slice, burger and arugula. Cover with top halves of rolls.

Makes 4 servings

French Onion Burgers

1 pound ground beef
1 can (10½ ounces) CAMPBELL'S® Condensed French Onion Soup
4 slices Swiss cheese
4 round hard rolls, split

1. Shape the beef into **4** (½-inch-thick) burgers.

2. Heat a 10-inch skillet over medium-high heat. Add the burgers and cook until they're well browned on both sides. Remove the burgers from the skillet. Pour off any fat.

3. Stir the soup in the skillet and heat to a boil. Return the burgers to the skillet. Reduce the heat to low. Cover and cook for 5 minutes or until the burgers are cooked through. Top the burgers with the cheese and cook until the cheese is melted. Serve the burgers in the rolls with the soup mixture. *Makes 4 servings*

Prep Time: 5 minutes
Cook Time: 20 minutes

Kitchen Tip: You can also serve these burgers in a bowl atop a mound of hot mashed potatoes with some of the onion gravy poured over.

Polynesian-Style Burgers

1 pound ground beef
¼ cup chopped onion
¼ cup chopped green bell pepper
3 teaspoons soy sauce, divided
½ teaspoon ground ginger, divided
¼ teaspoon garlic powder
1 can (about 5 ounces) pineapple slices
4 hamburger buns
Lettuce leaves

1. Preheat grill for direct cooking. Combine beef, onion, pepper, 2 teaspoons soy sauce, ¼ teaspoon ginger and garlic powder; mix lightly. Shape into 4 patties.

2. Drain pineapple; reserve ¼ cup juice. Combine juice, remaining 1 teaspoon soy sauce and ¼ teaspoon ginger in pie plate. Add pineapple; turn to coat.

3. Grill covered, over medium heat 8 to 10 minutes (uncovered 13 to 15 minutes) or until cooked through (160°F), turning once.

4. Grill pineapple until heated through. Serve burgers on buns; top with pineapple slices and lettuce. *Makes 4 servings*

quick 'n' easy

Spaghetti with Zesty Bolognese

 1 small onion, chopped
 ¼ cup KRAFT® Light Zesty Italian Reduced Fat Dressing
 1 pound extra lean ground beef
 1 can (15 ounces) tomato sauce
 1 can (14 ounces) diced tomatoes, undrained
 2 tablespoons PHILADELPHIA® Neufchâtel Cheese, ⅓ Less Fat than
     Cream Cheese
 12 ounces spaghetti, uncooked
 ¼ cup KRAFT® 100% Grated Parmesan Cheese

Cook onion in dressing in large skillet on medium heat. Increase heat to medium-high. Add meat; cook, stirring frequently, until browned. Stir in tomato sauce and tomatoes. Bring to boil. Reduce heat to medium-low; simmer 15 minutes. Remove from heat. Stir in Neufchâtel cheese until well blended.

Meanwhile, cook pasta as directed on package.

Spoon sauce over pasta. Sprinkle with Parmesan cheese.   *Makes 6 servings*

Prep Time: 10 minutes
Cook Time: 15 minutes

Sloppy Joe Burritos

1 pound ground beef
1 cup chopped bell pepper (red, green or a combination)
½ cup chopped onion
1 can (about 16 ounces) sloppy joe sauce
1 tablespoon cider vinegar
1 teaspoon sugar
1 teaspoon vegetable oil
¼ teaspoon salt
2 cups coleslaw mix
4 (7- to 8-inch) colored tortilla wraps

1. Cook beef, bell pepper and onion 6 to 8 minutes in large skillet over medium heat until beef is no longer pink, stirring to break up meat. Drain fat. Stir in sloppy joe sauce; cook over low heat about 3 minutes or until slightly thickened.

2. Whisk vinegar, sugar, oil and salt in medium bowl until well blended. Add coleslaw mix; toss to coat.

3. Divide meat mixture evenly among tortillas. Top meat with ½ cup coleslaw mixture. Roll up tortillas burrito-style, folding in sides to enclose filling. *Makes 4 servings*

Porcupine Meatballs

1 tablespoon butter or margarine
1 small onion, chopped
1 pound lean ground beef
1 cup MINUTE® White Rice, uncooked
1 egg, lightly beaten
1 packet (1½ ounces) meatloaf seasoning
¼ cup water
1 jar (14 ounces or larger) spaghetti sauce

Melt butter in small skillet over medium-high heat. Add onion; cook and stir until tender.

Place onion, beef, rice, egg and seasoning in large bowl. Add water; mix until well blended. Shape into medium-sized meatballs.

Pour spaghetti sauce into skillet. Bring to a boil. Add meatballs; return to a boil. Reduce heat to low; cover. Simmer 15 minutes or until meatballs are cooked through.   *Makes 4 servings*

Serving Suggestion: Round out each serving with ½ cup hot cooked rice and a serving of your favorite vegetables.

tip

To quickly shape uniform meatballs, place meat mixture on cutting board; pat evenly into a 1-inch-thick square. With sharp knife, cut meat into 1-inch squares; shape each square into a ball.

Thai-Style Beef with Pasta on Lettuce

3 tablespoons orange juice

2 tablespoons creamy peanut butter

2 tablespoons soy sauce

1 tablespoon natural rice vinegar

2 teaspoons grated fresh ginger

6 ounces uncooked whole wheat spaghetti, broken in half

½ pound ground beef

2 teaspoons minced garlic

2 cups (about 4 ounces) thinly sliced bok choy

½ cup (about 2 ounces) coarsely chopped carrot

4 green onions, cut into 1-inch pieces

¼ teaspoon crushed red pepper

6 pieces leaf lettuce

2 tablespoons (½ ounce) dry roasted peanuts

1. Process orange juice, peanut butter, soy sauce, vinegar and ginger in food processor or blender until nearly smooth. Set aside.

2. Cook spaghetti according to package directions, drain and set aside.

3. Meanwhile, cook beef and garlic 6 to 8 minutes in large nonstick skillet over medium-high heat until meat is brown, stirring to break up meat. Drain fat. Stir in bok choy, carrot, green onions and red pepper. Drizzle with orange juice mixture. Reduce heat to medium; cover and cook 2 minutes.

4. Add hot spaghetti; toss until combined. Place lettuce leaves on serving plates. Spoon noodle mixture onto leaves and sprinkle with peanuts. *Makes 6 servings*

Thai-Style Beef with Pasta on Lettuce

Caribbean Stuffed Plantains

        1 pound ground round beef
        3 tablespoons olive oil, divided
  1½ cups raw cubed NC sweet potatoes
        1 medium onion, chopped
        1 cup chopped green pepper
        ½ cup sliced celery
        1 large clove garlic, minced
        1 pound canned, chopped tomatoes
        1 tablespoon fresh oregano *or* 1 teaspoon dried oregano
        ½ teaspoon red pepper flakes
        ½ teaspoon seasoned salt
        2 tablespoons chopped parsley
        2 plantains
          Fresh oregano sprigs (optional)
          Pineapple wedges (optional)

1. In large skillet, brown beef in 1 tablespoon olive oil. Stir to break into bits. Add sweet potatoes, onion, pepper, celery and garlic. Sauté until vegetables are tender. Add tomatoes, oregano, red pepper, salt and parsley. Simmer 10 minutes to blend flavors.

2. In another skillet, heat remaining 2 tablespoons oil. Slice plantains lengthwise into 4 strips each; sauté in hot oil until golden. Remove from heat and shape into ring. Fasten ends with toothpick. Stand on edge on serving plate. Fill center with sweet potato filling. If desired, garnish with fresh sprigs of oregano and pineapple wedges.   *Makes 4 servings*

Favorite recipe from **North Carolina SweetPotato Commission**

Tex-Mex Meat Loaf Packets

4 sheets (18×12 inches) REYNOLDS WRAP® Non-Stick Foil
1 pound extra lean ground beef
¼ cup finely crushed tortilla chips
¼ cup finely chopped onion
2 teaspoons chili powder
2 teaspoons Worcestershire sauce
½ teaspoon garlic salt
¾ cup barbecue sauce, divided
1 package (10 ounces) frozen whole kernel corn *or* 1 can (15¼ ounces) whole kernel corn, drained

PREHEAT oven to 450°F or grill to medium-high. Combine lean ground beef, tortilla chips, onion, chili powder, Worcestershire sauce, garlic salt and ¼ cup barbecue sauce. Shape mixture into four meat loaves, flattening slightly.

CENTER one meat loaf on each sheet of Reynolds Wrap Non-Stick Foil with nonstick (dull) side toward food. Top with corn. Spoon remaining barbecue sauce over meat loaf and corn.

BRING up foil sides. Double fold top and ends to seal packet, leaving room for heat circulation inside. Repeat to make four packets.

BAKE 18 to 20 minutes on a cookie sheet in oven **OR GRILL** 12 to 14 minutes on covered grill.

Makes 4 servings

Prep Time: 10 minutes
Cook Time: 18 minutes

Spaghetti & Meatballs

Nonstick cooking spray
6 ounces uncooked multigrain or whole wheat spaghetti
¾ pound ground beef
¼ pound turkey Italian sausage, casing removed
1 egg white
2 tablespoons plain dry bread crumbs
1 teaspoon dried oregano
2 cups tomato-basil pasta sauce
3 tablespoons chopped fresh basil
2 tablespoons grated Parmesan cheese

1. Preheat oven to 450°F. Coat baking sheet with cooking spray. Cook spaghetti according to package directions.

2. Combine beef, sausage, egg white, bread crumbs and oregano in medium bowl; mix well. Shape mixture into 16 (1½-inch) meatballs. Place on prepared baking sheet; coat with cooking spray. Bake 12 minutes, turning once.

3. Pour pasta sauce into large skillet; add meatballs. Cook and stir over medium heat 9 minutes or until sauce is heated through and meatballs are cooked through (160°F). Drain spaghetti; divide among plates. Top with meatballs and sauce; sprinkle with basil and Parmesan.

Makes 4 servings

Beefy Pasta Skillet

1 pound ground beef

1 medium onion, chopped (about ½ cup)

1 can (10¾ ounces) CAMPBELL'S® Condensed Tomato Soup (Regular or Healthy Request®)

¼ cup water

1 tablespoon Worcestershire sauce

½ cup shredded Cheddar cheese

2 cups cooked corkscrew-shaped pasta (rotini) or elbow pasta

1. Cook the beef and onion in a 10-inch skillet over medium-high heat until the beef is well browned, stirring often to separate the meat. Pour off any fat.

2. Stir the soup, water, Worcestershire, cheese and pasta in the skillet and cook until the mixture is hot and bubbling.   *Makes 4 servings*

Prep Time: 5 minutes
Cook Time: 15 minutes

tip

Skillet dishes are a fast and easy way to make a meal. They require just a few ingredients and use only one pan, making cleanup a breeze and leaving plenty of time to enjoy your meal.

Salisbury Steaks with Mushroom-Wine Sauce

1 pound ground beef
¾ teaspoon garlic salt or seasoned salt
¼ teaspoon black pepper
2 tablespoons butter or margarine
1 package (8 ounces) sliced mushrooms
2 tablespoons sweet vermouth or ruby port wine
1 jar (12 ounces) *or* 1 can (10½ ounces) beef gravy

1. Heat large nonstick skillet over medium-high heat. Combine beef, garlic salt and pepper in medium bowl; mix well. Shape mixture into 4 oval patties.

2. Place patties in skillet; cook 3 minutes per side or until browned. Transfer to plate. Pour off drippings.

3. Melt butter in same skillet; add mushrooms. Cook and stir 2 minutes. Add vermouth; cook 1 minute. Add gravy; mix well.

4. Return patties to skillet; simmer uncovered over medium heat, stirring occasionally 2 minutes or until cooked through (160°F). *Makes 4 servings*

Prep and Cook Time: 20 minutes

Note: For a special touch, sprinkle the cooked steaks with chopped fresh parsley or chives.

Cheesy Cheeseburger Mac

1 pound ground beef
1¼ cups water
¾ cup milk
⅓ cup ketchup
1 package (12 ounces) VELVEETA® Shells & Cheese Dinner
1 large tomato, chopped

BROWN meat in large skillet; drain.

ADD water, milk and ketchup; mix well. Bring to a boil. Stir in Shell Macaroni; return to boil. Reduce heat to medium-low; cover. Simmer 10 minutes or until macaroni is tender.

STIR in Cheese Sauce and tomato until well blended. Cook until heated through, stirring occasionally.
Makes 4 servings

Prep Time: 10 minutes
Total Time: 30 minutes

Serving Suggestion: Serve with a crisp mixed green salad tossed with your favorite KRAFT® Dressing.

mexican fiesta

Mexican Picadillo

     1 pound lean ground beef
 ¾ cup diced onion
     1 can (28 ounces) plum tomatoes, drained
 ½ cup seedless raisins
 ½ cup B&G® Pimento-Stuffed Olives, sliced
     2 tablespoons REGINA® White Wine Vinegar
     1 teaspoon ground cinnamon
     1 teaspoon ground cumin
 ¾ teaspoon ORTEGA® Chili Seasoning Mix
        Salt and black pepper, to taste
 10 ORTEGA® Taco Shells
     1 cup shredded Cheddar cheese

Preheat oven to 225°F. Brown beef in medium skillet over medium heat. Add onions; cook and stir 5 minutes or until softened. Drain excess fat and discard. Add tomatoes, breaking up with wooden spoon. Stir in raisins, olives, vinegar, cinnamon, cumin, seasoning mix, salt and pepper. Bring mixture to a boil. Reduce heat; simmer uncovered, 10 minutes.

Place taco shells on baking sheet; bake 5 to 10 minutes or until warmed. Fill shells with beef mixture and sprinkle with cheese. *Makes 4 to 5 servings*

Prep Time: 10 minutes
Start to Finish: 25 minutes

Tip: If you prefer soft flour tortillas, use them instead. Just spoon the filling down the center of the tortillas, add the cheese, roll up and enjoy!

Overstuffed Peppers, Mexican Style

10 ounces ground beef

½ cup finely chopped onion

1 can (about 4 ounces) mild chopped green chiles

½ cup frozen corn kernels

½ cup tomato sauce, divided

¼ cup cornmeal

½ teaspoon ground cumin

½ teaspoon salt

2 large green bell peppers, split in half lengthwise, seeds and stem removed (about 8 ounces each)

⅔ cup (2 ounces) shredded sharp Cheddar cheese

1. Preheat oven to 375°F.

2. Brown beef 6 to 8 minutes in large skillet over medium-high heat, stirring to break up meat. Drain fat. Stir in onion, chiles, corn, ¼ cup tomato sauce, cornmeal, cumin and salt.

3. Arrange peppers, cut side up, in 12×8-inch baking pan. Spoon equal amounts of beef mixture into each pepper half. Spoon remaining ¼ cup tomato sauce evenly over each pepper. Bake uncovered, 35 minutes or until peppers are tender.

4. Sprinkle each pepper with equal amounts of cheese. Serve immediately.

Makes 4 servings

tip

To freeze, place pepper halves in resealable food storage bags. Release any excess air from bags; seal. Freeze bags flat for easier storage and faster thawing. To reheat, open bags and place on microwaveable plate. Microwave on HIGH 3 to 3½ minutes or until heated through.

Soft Tacos

    1 pound ground beef
    1 package (1.25 ounces) taco seasoning mix
    ¾ cup water
    8 flour tortillas (8-inch), warmed
    1 cup PACE® Picante Sauce
    1 cup shredded iceberg lettuce
    1 cup shredded Cheddar cheese (4 ounces)

1. Cook the beef in a 10-inch skillet over medium-high heat until the beef is well browned, stirring frequently to separate meat. Pour off any fat.

2. Stir the taco seasoning mix and water into the skillet. Heat to a boil. Reduce the heat to low. Cook for 5 minutes.

3. Spoon about ¼ cup beef mixture down center of each tortilla. Divide the picante sauce, lettuce and cheese among the tortillas. Fold the tortilla around the filling. Serve with additional picante sauce.   *Makes 8 tacos*

Prep and Cook Time: 15 minutes

Layered Beef Enchiladas

    Red Chili Sauce (page 118)
    1 pound ground beef
    1 cup finely chopped white onion
    1 clove garlic, minced
    ½ teaspoon salt
    ¾ cup vegetable oil, divided
    12 (6-inch) corn tortillas
    2 cups (8 ounces) shredded Cheddar cheese
    ⅔ cup chopped pitted black olives
    1½ cups shredded iceberg lettuce and chopped fresh cilantro (optional)

1. Prepare Red Chili Sauce.

2. Brown beef 6 to 8 minutes in large skillet over medium-high heat, stirring to break up meat. Drain fat. Add onion; cook and stir 4 minutes or until softened.

continued on page 118

Layered Beef Enchiladas, continued

3. Stir in garlic, salt and 1 cup Red Chili Sauce; mix well. Bring to a boil over medium heat. Reduce heat to low. Simmer uncovered, 5 minutes or until most liquid is evaporated, stirring frequently.

4. Heat oil in medium skillet over medium heat. Fry tortillas, 1 at a time, 10 to 20 seconds or until limp and blistered, turning once. Drain on paper towels. Remove and discard oil.

5. Heat remaining $1^1/_2$ cups Red Chili Sauce in medium skillet over medium heat. Remove from heat.

6. Dip 1 tortilla into sauce with tongs to coat; remove. Drain excess sauce; place on individual broiler-proof plate. Spread about $^1/_4$ cup meat filling on tortilla; sprinkle with 2 tablespoons cheese and 1 tablespoon olives. Repeat, making two more layers. Repeat with remaining ingredients.

7. Place enchiladas in broiler 4 inches from heat. Broil 3 minutes or until cheese is melted. Sprinkle with remaining olives. Garnish with lettuce and cilantro. *Makes 4 servings*

Red Chili Sauce

3 ounces dried ancho chiles (about 5), toasted, seeded, deveined and rinsed
$2^1/_2$ **cups boiling water**
  2 tablespoons vegetable oil
  2 tablespoons tomato paste
  1 clove garlic, minced
$^1/_2$ **teaspoon salt**
$^1/_2$ **teaspoon dried oregano**
$^1/_4$ **teaspoon ground cumin**
$^1/_4$ **teaspoon ground coriander**

1. Place chiles in medium bowl; cover with boiling water. Let stand 1 hour.

2. Place chiles along with soaking water in blender; process until smooth.

3. Pour into medium saucepan; whisk in oil, tomato paste, garlic, salt, oregano, cumin and coriander. Bring to a boil over medium-high heat. Reduce heat to low. Cover and simmer 10 minutes, stirring occasionally. *Makes about $2^1/_2$ cups*

Note: Sauce can be refrigerated covered, up to 3 days or frozen up to 1 month.

Cheesy Chimichangas

1½ **pounds lean ground beef**
2 **large onions, chopped**
2 **teaspoons garlic salt**
½ **teaspoon black pepper**
8 **(8-inch) ORTEGA® Soft Flour Tortillas**
2 **tablespoons vegetable oil, divided**
1 **jar (16 ounces) ORTEGA® Salsa, any variety, divided**
2 **cups (8 ounces) shredded Cheddar cheese, divided**
2 **cups (8 ounces) shredded Monterey Jack cheese, divided**
   Shredded lettuce
   Chopped tomatoes
1 **jar (11.5 ounces) ORTEGA® Guacamole Style Dip**

Preheat oven to 450°F. Grease or lightly coat 13×9-inch baking dish with nonstick cooking spray; set aside.

Cook and stir beef and onions in large skillet over medium-high heat until no longer pink. Drain and discard fat. Stir in garlic salt and pepper.

Brush one side of each tortilla with oil. Spoon ¼ cup beef mixture off-center on oiled side of each tortilla. Top each with 1 tablespoon salsa, 1 tablespoon Cheddar cheese and 1 tablespoon Monterey Jack cheese. Fold ends of tortilla to middle, then roll tightly around mixture. Secure with toothpick. Place in prepared baking dish. Repeat with remaining tortillas. Brush tops with remaining oil.

Bake, uncovered, 10 to 15 minutes or until lightly browned. Sprinkle with remaining cheeses. Bake 2 to 3 minutes longer or until cheese is melted. Remove toothpicks.

Serve warm on bed of lettuce and tomatoes. Spoon remaining salsa over chimichangas. Serve with guacamole.   *Makes 8 servings*

Prep Time: 25 minutes
Start to Finish: 40 minutes

Chili-Stuffed Poblano Peppers

1 pound ground beef
4 large poblano peppers
1 can (about 15 ounces) chili beans
1 can (about 14 ounces) tomatoes with chiles in sauce, undrained
1 tablespoon Mexican adobo seasoning
⅔ cup shredded Mexican cheese blend or Monterey Jack cheese

1. Preheat broiler. Bring 2 quarts water to a boil in 3-quart saucepan. Meanwhile, brown beef 6 to 8 minutes in large nonstick skillet over medium-high heat, stirring to break up meat. Drain fat.

2. Cut peppers in half lengthwise; remove stems and seeds. Add 4 pepper halves to boiling water; cook 3 minutes or until bright green and slightly softened. Drain upside down on plate. Repeat with remaining 4 halves. Arrange peppers, cut side up, in 13×9-inch baking dish.

3. Add beans, tomatoes and Mexican seasoning to ground beef. Cook and stir over medium heat 5 minutes or until mixture thickens slightly.

4. Divide chili mixture evenly among peppers; top with cheese. Broil 6 inches from heat 1 minute or until cheese is melted. Serve immediately. *Makes 4 servings*

Prep and Cook Time: 26 minutes

Serving Suggestion: Serve with pico de gallo.

tip

Poblano peppers are very dark green, large, triangular-shaped chiles with pointed ends. Their flavor ranges from mild to quite hot. To avoid irritating the skin, wear rubber gloves when handling and do not touch your eyes.

Chili-Stuffed Poblano Peppers

Fiesta Taco Salad

1 pound ground beef

2 tablespoons chili powder

1 can (10¾ ounces) CAMPBELL'S® Condensed Tomato Soup (Regular or Healthy Request®)

8 cups salad greens torn into bite-size pieces

2 cups tortilla chips

Chopped tomato

Sliced green onions

Shredded Cheddar cheese

Sliced pitted ripe olives

1. In medium skillet over medium-high heat, cook beef and chili powder until beef is browned, stirring to separate meat. Pour off fat.

2. Add soup. Reduce heat to low and heat through.

3. Arrange salad greens and chips on platter. Spoon meat mixture over salad greens. Top with tomato, onions, cheese and olives. *Makes 4 servings*

Prep Time: 10 minutes
Cook Time: 15 minutes

Beefy Nacho Crescent Bake

1 pound ground beef
½ cup chopped onion
¼ teaspoon salt
⅛ teaspoon black pepper
1 tablespoon chili powder
1 teaspoon ground cumin
1 teaspoon dried oregano
1 can (10¾ ounces) condensed nacho cheese soup, undiluted
1 cup milk
1 package (8 count) refrigerated crescent roll dough
¼ cup (1 ounce) shredded Cheddar cheese
Chopped fresh cilantro (optional)
Guacamole (optional)

1. Preheat oven to 375°F. Spray 13×9-inch baking dish with nonstick cooking spray.

2. Season beef and onion with salt and pepper. Brown 6 to 8 minutes in large skillet over medium-high heat, stirring to break up meat. Drain fat. Stir in chili powder, cumin and oregano. Cook and stir 2 minutes; remove from heat. Combine soup and milk in medium bowl; spread evenly into prepared dish.

3. Separate crescent dough into 4 rectangles; press perforations together firmly. Roll each rectangle to 8×4 inches. Cut each rectangle in half crosswise to form 8 (4-inch) squares.

4. Spoon about ¼ cup beef mixture into center of each square. Lift 4 corners of dough up over filling to meet in center; pinch and twist firmly to seal. Place squares in prepared dish.

5. Bake uncovered, 20 to 25 minutes or until crusts are golden brown. Sprinkle cheese over squares. Bake 5 minutes or until cheese melts. Sprinkle with cilantro and serve with guacamole, if desired.

Makes 4 servings

Smothered Beef and Bean Burritos

1 can (10¾ ounces) condensed cream of mushroom soup

1 can (10¾ ounces) condensed Cheddar cheese soup

½ cup sour cream

1 tablespoon olive oil

1 pound lean ground beef

1 onion, diced

¾ cup water

1 ORTEGA® Soft Taco Kit—includes 10 soft flour tortillas, 1 packet (1.25 ounces) taco seasoning mix and 1 packet (3 ounces) taco sauce

1 cup ORTEGA® Refried Beans

2 tablespoons chopped fresh cilantro

¼ cup diced tomato

Preheat oven to 350°F. Lightly coat 13×9-inch baking dish with nonstick cooking spray. Combine soups and sour cream in small bowl; set aside.

Heat oil in skillet over medium-high heat. Add beef and onion. Cook and stir 5 minutes or until beef is no longer pink. Drain and discard fat. Add water and seasoning mix from Soft Taco Kit. Cook and stir 3 minutes. Stir in refried beans.

Wrap tortillas from Soft Taco Kit with clean, lightly moistened cloth or paper towels. Microwave on HIGH (100% power) 1 minute or until hot and pliable.

Divide beef mixture evenly among tortillas. Fold ends of tortilla to middle, then roll tightly around mixture. Place in baking dish, seam side down. Repeat with remaining tortillas.

Spread soup mixture evenly over tortillas. Bake 22 to 25 minutes or until heated through. Garnish with taco sauce from Soft Taco Kit, cilantro and tomatoes.   *Makes 10 burritos*

Prep Time: 10 minutes
Start to Finish: 40 minutes

Tip: For a more complete meal, add chopped cooked broccoli, carrots or your favorite vegetable to the filling mixture.

Fiesta Beef Enchiladas

1 pound ground beef
½ cup sliced green onions
2 teaspoons minced garlic
1½ cups chopped tomatoes, divided
1 cup cooked white or brown rice
1 cup (4 ounces) shredded Mexican cheese blend or Cheddar cheese, divided
¾ cup frozen corn, thawed
½ cup salsa or picante sauce
12 (6- to 7-inch) corn tortillas
1 can (10 ounces) enchilada sauce
1 cup shredded romaine lettuce

1. Preheat oven to 375°F. Spray 13×9-inch baking dish with nonstick cooking spray.

2. Brown beef 6 to 8 minutes in medium nonstick skillet over medium-high heat, stirring to break up meat. Drain fat. Add green onions and garlic; cook and stir 2 minutes.

3. Add 1 cup tomatoes, rice, ½ cup cheese, corn and salsa to meat mixture; mix well. Spoon mixture down center of tortillas. Roll up; place seam side down in prepared dish. Spoon enchilada sauce evenly over enchiladas.

4. Cover with foil; bake 20 minutes or until heated through. Sprinkle with remaining ½ cup cheese; bake 5 minutes or until cheese melts. Top with lettuce and remaining ½ cup tomatoes.

Makes 6 servings

Prep Time: 15 minutes
Cook Time: 35 minutes

casserole creations

Layered Pasta Casserole

8 ounces uncooked penne pasta

8 ounces Italian sausage, casings removed

8 ounces ground beef

1 jar (about 26 ounces) pasta sauce

1 package (10 ounces) frozen chopped spinach, thawed and squeezed dry

2 cups (8 ounces) shredded mozzarella cheese, divided

1 cup ricotta cheese

½ cup grated Parmesan cheese

1 egg

2 tablespoons chopped fresh basil *or* 2 teaspoons dried basil

1 teaspoon salt

1. Preheat oven to 350°F. Spray 13×9-inch baking dish with nonstick cooking spray. Cook pasta according to package directions; drain. Transfer to prepared dish.

2. Brown sausage and ground beef 6 to 8 minutes in large skillet over medium-high heat, stirring to break up meat. Drain fat. Add pasta sauce; mix well. Add half of meat sauce to pasta; toss to coat.

3. Combine spinach, 1 cup mozzarella, ricotta, Parmesan, egg, basil and salt in medium bowl. Spoon small mounds of spinach mixture over pasta mixture; spread evenly with back of spoon. Top with remaining meat sauce; sprinkle with remaining 1 cup mozzarella. Bake uncovered, 30 minutes.   *Makes 6 to 8 servings*

Garlic Mashed Potatoes & Beef Bake

1 pound ground beef

1 can (10¾ ounces) CAMPBELL'S® Condensed Cream of Mushroom with Roasted Garlic Soup

1 tablespoon Worcestershire sauce

1 bag (16 ounces) frozen vegetable combination (broccoli, cauliflower, carrots), thawed*

2 cups water

3 tablespoons butter

¾ cup milk

2 cups instant mashed potato flakes

*Or any frozen vegetable combination.

1. Heat the oven to 400°F. Cook the beef in a 10-inch skillet over medium-high heat until it's well browned, stirring often to separate meat. Pour off any fat.

2. Stir the beef, ½ **can** soup, Worcestershire and vegetables in a 2-quart shallow baking dish.

3. Heat the water, butter and remaining soup in a 3-quart saucepan over medium heat to a boil. Remove the saucepan from the heat. Stir in the milk. Stir in the potatoes. Spoon the potatoes over the beef mixture.

4. Bake for 20 minutes or until the potatoes are lightly browned.   *Makes 4 servings*

Prep Time: 15 minutes
Bake Time: 20 minutes

Empanada Pie

1 pound ground beef
1 small onion, chopped
1 package (1¼ ounces) taco seasoning mix
1 can (about 8 ounces) tomato sauce
¼ cup raisins
2 teaspoons dark brown sugar
1 package (8 count) refrigerated crescent roll dough
Sliced green onion (optional)

1. Preheat oven to 375°F. Grease 10-inch shallow round baking dish or deep-dish pie plate.

2. Brown beef and onion 6 to 8 minutes in large skillet over medium-high heat, stirring to break up meat. Drain fat. Sprinkle taco seasoning over beef mixture. Add tomato sauce, raisins and sugar. Reduce heat to low; cook 2 to 3 minutes.

3. Spoon beef mixture into prepared dish. Unroll crescent dough; separate into triangles. Arrange 5 triangles on top of beef mixture in a spiral with points of dough towards center. Do not seal dough pieces together. Reserve remaining dough for another use.

4. Bake 13 to 17 minutes or until dough is puffed and golden brown. Garnish with green onion.

Makes 4 to 6 servings

tip

The next time you are making a casserole, assemble and bake two. Allow one to cool completely, then wrap it in heavy-duty foil and freeze it for another meal. To reheat, unwrap it and microwave covered, on HIGH for 20 to 30 minutes, stirring once or twice during cooking. Allow to stand for about 5 minutes.

Chili Beef and Corn Casserole

¾ **pound ground beef**

¼ **cup salsa**

2 **teaspoons chili powder**

1½ **teaspoons ground cumin**

2 **cups frozen corn, thawed**

2 **ounces chopped collard greens, about ½-inch pieces (1 cup packed)**

½ **cup sour cream**

¼ **cup (1 ounce) shredded sharp Cheddar cheese**

1. Preheat oven 350°F.

2. Brown beef 6 to 8 minutes in large skillet over medium-high heat; stirring to break up meat. Drain fat. Add salsa, chili powder and cumin; cook and stir 1 minute. Remove from heat.

3. Coat 8-inch square baking pan with nonstick cooking spray. Combine corn and collard greens in prepared pan. Spoon beef mixture evenly over vegetables; cover with foil.

4. Bake 25 minutes or until greens are tender. Top each serving evenly with sour cream and cheese.

Makes 4 servings

Beef & Zucchini Quiche

   1 unbaked 9-inch pie crust
½ pound ground beef
   1 medium zucchini, shredded
   3 green onions, sliced
¼ cup sliced mushrooms
   1 tablespoon all-purpose flour
   1 cup milk
   3 eggs, beaten
¾ cup (3 ounces) shredded Swiss cheese
1½ teaspoons chopped fresh thyme *or* ½ teaspoon dried thyme
½ teaspoon salt
   Dash black pepper
   Dash ground red pepper

1. Preheat oven to 475°F.

2. Spray pie plate with nonstick cooking spray. Place crust in prepared pan. Line pie crust with foil; fill with dried beans or rice. Bake 8 minutes. Remove from oven; carefully remove foil and beans. Return pie crust to oven. Continue baking 4 minutes; set aside. *Reduce oven temperature to 375°F.*

3. Brown beef 6 to 8 minutes in medium skillet over medium-high heat, stirring to break up meat. Drain fat. Add zucchini, green onions and mushrooms; cook, stirring occasionally, until vegetables are tender. Stir in flour; cook 2 minutes, stirring constantly. Remove from heat.

4. Combine milk, eggs, cheese, thyme, salt, black pepper and red pepper in medium bowl. Stir into ground beef mixture; pour filling into crust. Bake 35 minutes or until knife inserted near center comes out clean.

Makes 6 servings

Pizza Roll-Ups

½ pound lean ground beef
1 small onion, chopped
¾ teaspoon garlic salt
¼ teaspoon crushed red pepper flakes
1 jar (28 ounces) pasta sauce with mushrooms, divided
2 cups (8 ounces) SARGENTO® Fancy Shredded 6 Cheese Italian Cheese, divided
8 long (6 ounces) lasagna noodles, cooked and drained

BROWN ground beef and onion in large skillet. Pour off drippings. Sprinkle meat mixture with garlic salt and pepper flakes. Remove from heat; stir in ½ cup pasta sauce and 1½ cups cheese.

SPOON 1 cup pasta sauce into 2-quart rectangular baking dish. Spoon ¼ cup meat mixture down center of each lasagna noodle; roll up and place, seam-side down, in baking dish. Spoon remaining sauce over roll-ups.

COVER with foil; bake in preheated 375°F oven 35 minutes or until heated through. Remove from oven; uncover and sprinkle with remaining cheese. Let stand 5 minutes before serving.

Makes 8 servings

Prep Time: 20 minutes
Cook Time: 35 minutes

tip

Glass and ceramic bakeware absorb heat more slowly and hold heat better than metal. Therefore, both glass and ceramic make good choices for casseroles and acidic dishes.

Meat Crust Pie

1 pound ground beef
2 cans (about 8 ounces each) tomato sauce, divided
½ cup seasoned dry bread crumbs
½ cup chopped green bell pepper, divided
¼ cup minced onion
1 teaspoon salt, divided
⅛ teaspoon dried oregano
⅛ teaspoon black pepper
1 cup water
1⅓ cups uncooked instant rice
1 cup (4 ounces) shredded Cheddar cheese, divided

1. Preheat oven to 350°F. Combine beef, ½ cup tomato sauce, bread crumbs, ¼ cup bell pepper, onion, ½ teaspoon salt, oregano and black pepper in large bowl; mix well. Pat onto bottom and up side of ungreased 9-inch deep-dish pie plate.

2. Bring water and remaining ½ teaspoon salt to a boil in medium saucepan. Stir in rice; cover and remove from heat. Let stand 5 minutes or until water is absorbed. Add remaining 1½ cups tomato sauce, ½ cup cheese and remaining ¼ cup bell pepper to rice; mix well. Spoon rice mixture into meat shell. Cover with foil; bake 25 minutes.

3. Remove from oven and drain fat carefully, holding pan lid over top to keep pie from sliding. Top with remaining ½ cup cheese. Bake uncovered, 10 to 15 minutes or until cheese melts. Carefully drain fat again. Cut into wedges to serve. *Makes 8 servings*

Cheesy Italian Pasta Bake

What You Need

1½ **cups wagon wheel pasta, uncooked**

1 **pound extra lean ground beef**

1 **large carrot, shredded (about 1 cup)**

1 **large zucchini, shredded (about 1 cup)**

1 **red pepper, chopped**

1 **can (8 ounces) pizza sauce**

½ **pound (8 ounces) VELVEETA® 2% Milk Pasteurized Prepared Cheese Product, cut into ½-inch cubes**

½ **cup KRAFT® Grated Parmesan Cheese**

Make It

1. HEAT oven to 350°F. Cook pasta as directed on package. Meanwhile, brown meat in large nonstick skillet on medium-high heat; drain. Stir in vegetables and sauce; cook 5 minutes or until vegetables are tender. Drain pasta. Add to meat mixture along with VELVEETA®; mix well.

2. SPOON into 8-inch square baking dish sprayed with cooking spray; sprinkle with Parmesan.

3. BAKE 15 to 20 minutes or until heated through.   *Makes 6 servings*

Prep Time: 25 minutes
Total Time: 45 minutes

Beefy Mexican Lasagna

1½ pounds ground beef sirloin (95% lean)
2 cans (10 ounces each) mild enchilada sauce
1 can (15 ounces) black beans, rinsed, drained
1½ cups frozen corn
1 teaspoon ground cumin
9 corn tortillas
1½ cups shredded Mexican cheese blend
Crunchy Tortilla Strips (recipe follows, optional)
½ cup chopped tomato
2 tablespoons chopped fresh cilantro

1. Heat oven to 350°F. Heat large nonstick skillet over medium heat until hot. Add ground beef; cook 8 to 10 minutes, breaking into crumbles and stirring occasionally. Remove from skillet with slotted spoon; pour off drippings. Return beef to skillet; stir in 1 can enchilada sauce, black beans, corn and cumin; bring to a boil. Reduce heat; simmer 5 minutes, stirring occasionally.

2. Spray 11×7 inch baking dish with nonstick cooking spray. Arrange 3 tortillas in dish, cutting 1 as needed to cover bottom. Spread ¼ cup remaining enchilada sauce over tortillas; cover with ⅓ beef mixture, then ⅓ cheese. Repeat layers twice, omitting final cheese layer. Pour remaining enchilada sauce over top.

3. Cover with aluminum foil. Bake in 350°F oven 30 minutes. Remove foil; sprinkle with remaining ½ cup cheese. Bake, uncovered, 5 minutes or until cheese is melted. Top with tortilla strips, if desired, tomato and cilantro. *Makes 6 to 8 servings*

Prep and Cook Time: 45 minutes

Crunchy Tortilla Strips: Heat oven to 400°F. Cut 1 corn tortilla in half, then crosswise into ¼-inch-wide strips. Place strips in single layer on baking sheet. Spray lightly with nonstick cooking spray. Bake 4 to 8 minutes or until crisp.

Cook's Tip: Lasagna may be made up to 24 hours ahead through step 2; cover and refrigerate. Increase baking time from 30 minutes to 45 minutes.

Cook's Tip: Cooking times are for fresh or thoroughly thawed ground beef. Ground beef should be cooked to an internal temperature of 160°F. Color is not a reliable indicator of ground beef doneness.

Favorite recipe from **Courtesy The Beef Checkoff**

amazing chilis

HERSHEY'S Secret Ingredient Chili

¼ **cup vegetable oil**

1½ **cups chopped onion**

2 **pounds lean ground beef**

2 **tablespoons HERSHEY'S Cocoa**

2 **tablespoons chili powder**

2 **teaspoons ground cayenne pepper**

1 **teaspoon salt**

½ **teaspoon ground allspice**

½ **teaspoon ground cinnamon**

2 **cans (28 ounces each) whole tomatoes, undrained**

1 **can (12 ounces) tomato paste**

1 **cup water**

2 **cans (about 15 ounces each) red kidney beans, drained (optional)**

   Additional chopped onion (optional)

   Shredded Cheddar cheese (optional)

1. In 5-quart saucepan, over medium heat, heat oil; add onion. Cook, stirring frequently, 3 minutes or until tender. Add meat; cook until brown. Drain.

2. Stir in cocoa, seasonings, tomatoes with liquid, tomato paste and water; heat to boiling. Reduce heat; simmer 30 minutes.

3. Serve plain, topped with beans, sprinkled with additional chopped onion, topped with cheese or all of the above.

Makes 12 servings

Baked Black Bean Chili

1½ **pounds ground beef**
¼ **cup chopped onion**
¼ **cup chopped green bell pepper**
1 **can (about 15 ounces) black beans, rinsed and drained**
1 **can (about 14 ounces) diced tomatoes with green chiles**
1 **can (about 14 ounces) beef broth**
1 **can (about 8 ounces) tomato sauce**
5 **tablespoons chili powder**
1 **tablespoon sugar**
1 **tablespoon ground cumin**
1 **teaspoon dried minced onion**
⅛ **teaspoon garlic powder**
⅛ **teaspoon ground ginger**
2 **cups (8 ounces) shredded Mexican cheese blend**

1. Preheat oven to 350°F. Cook beef, chopped onion and bell pepper 6 to 8 minutes in large skillet over medium-high heat, stirring to break up meat. Drain fat. Transfer to 4-quart casserole.

2. Stir in beans, tomatoes, broth, tomato sauce, chili powder, sugar, cumin, dried onion, garlic powder and ginger. Cover and bake 30 minutes, stirring every 10 minutes. Uncover; top with cheese. Bake about 5 minutes or until cheese begins to melt.   *Makes 6 to 8 servings*

Chorizo Chili

1 **pound ground beef**
8 **ounces bulk raw chorizo** *or* ½ **package (15 ounces) raw chorizo**
1 **can (about 16 ounces) chili beans in chili sauce**
2 **cans (about 14 ounces each) zesty chili-style diced tomatoes**

Slow Cooker Directions
1. Place beef and chorizo in slow cooker. Stir to break up well.

2. Stir in beans and tomatoes. Cover; cook on LOW 7 hours. Skim off and discard excess fat before serving.   *Makes 6 servings*

Prep Time: 5 minutes
Cook Time: 7 hours

Serving Suggestion: Top with sour cream or shredded cheese.

Baked Black Bean Chili

Cincinnati Chili

1½ **pounds ground beef**

   2 **large onions, chopped (about 2 cups)**

¼ **teaspoon garlic powder** *or* **2 cloves garlic, minced**

   2 **teaspoons chili powder**

¼ **teaspoon ground cinnamon**

      Dash ground cloves

   4 **cups CAMPBELL'S® Tomato Juice**

   2 **cans (about 15 ounces each) kidney beans, drained**

      Hot cooked spaghetti, shredded cheese and chopped onion

1. Cook the beef, onions and garlic powder in 2 batches in a 6-quart saucepot over medium-high heat until the beef is well browned, stirring frequently to separate meat. Pour off any fat.

2. Add the chili powder, cinnamon and cloves. Cook and stir for 2 minutes. Add the tomato juice. Heat to a boil. Reduce the heat to low. Cover and cook for 30 minutes.

3. Stir in the beans. Cover and cook for 15 minutes, stirring occasionally. Serve over spaghetti topped with shredded cheese and onion.   *Makes 8 servings*

Hands On Time: 10 minutes
Cook Time: 1 hour

Have Your Way with Cincinnati Chili: Serve it with just pasta (two-way) or add your choice of toppings cheese, beans, onions or all three (five-way).

Best Ever Chili

1½ **pounds ground beef**
1 **cup chopped onion**
2 **cans (about 15 ounces each) kidney beans, 1 cup juice reserved**
1½ **pounds plum tomatoes, diced**
1 **can (about 15 ounces) tomato paste**
3 **to 6 tablespoons chili powder**
Sour cream
Green onion, sliced

Slow Cooker Directions

1. Cook beef and onion 6 to 8 minutes in large skillet over medium-high heat, stirring to break up meat. Drain fat. Transfer to slow cooker.

2. Add kidney beans, tomatoes, tomato paste, reserved bean juice and chili powder to slow cooker; mix well. Cover; cook on LOW 10 to 12 hours. Top with sour cream and green onion.

Makes 8 servings

Chili Beef Express

1 **pound ground beef (95% lean)**
¼ **teaspoon salt**
¼ **teaspoon pepper**
1 **can (15½ ounces) chili beans in chili sauce, undrained**
1 **can (14½ ounces) chili-style chunky tomatoes, undrained**
1 **cup frozen corn**
2 **tablespoons chopped fresh cilantro**

1. Brown ground beef in large nonstick skillet over medium heat 8 to 10 minutes or until beef is not pink, breaking up into ³/₄-inch crumbles. Pour off drippings; season with salt and pepper.

2. Stir in beans, tomatoes and corn; bring to a boil. Reduce heat; cover and simmer 10 minutes. Sprinkle with cilantro before serving.

Makes 4 servings

Prep and Cook Time: 25 minutes

Cook's Tip: This recipe may be doubled; prepare in stockpot instead of skillet.

Favorite recipe from **Courtesy The Beef Checkoff**

Chili

3 pounds ground beef
2 cans (about 14 ounces each) diced tomatoes
2 cans (about 14 ounces each) chili beans, undrained
2 cups sliced onions
1 can (about 12 ounces) corn, drained
1 cup chopped green bell pepper
1 can (about 8 ounces) tomato sauce
3 tablespoons chili powder
1 teaspoon garlic powder
½ teaspoon ground cumin
½ teaspoon dried oregano

Slow Cooker Directions

1. Brown beef 6 to 8 minutes in large skillet over medium-high heat, stirring to break up meat. Drain fat. Transfer beef to 5-quart slow cooker.

2. Add tomatoes, beans, onions, corn, bell pepper, tomato sauce, chili powder, garlic powder, cumin and oregano. Stir well. Cover; cook on LOW 4 hours.   *Makes 6 servings*

Prep Time: 15 minutes

Classic Chili

1½ pounds ground beef
1½ cups chopped onion
1 cup chopped green bell pepper
2 cloves garlic, minced
3 cans (about 15 ounces each) dark red kidney beans, rinsed and drained
2 cans (about 15 ounces each) tomato sauce
1 can (about 14 ounces) diced tomatoes
2 to 3 teaspoons chili powder
1 to 2 teaspoons dry hot mustard
¾ teaspoon dried basil
½ teaspoon black pepper
1 to 2 dried hot chile peppers (optional)

Slow Cooker Directions

1. Cook beef, onion, bell pepper and garlic 6 to 8 minutes in large skillet or until meat is browned and onion is tender. Drain fat. Transfer beef mixture to 5-quart slow cooker.

2. Add beans, tomato sauce, tomatoes, chili powder, mustard, basil, black pepper and chile peppers, if desired; mix well. Cover; cook on LOW 8 to 10 hours or on HIGH 4 to 5 hours.

3. Remove chile peppers before serving.   *Makes 6 servings*

Easy Slow-Cooked Chili

2 pounds lean ground beef
2 tablespoons chili powder
1 tablespoon ground cumin
1 can (28 ounces) crushed tomatoes in purée, undrained
1 can (15 ounces) red kidney beans, drained and rinsed
1 cup water
2 cups *French's*® French Fried Onions,* divided
¼ cup *Frank's*® *RedHot*® Original Cayenne Pepper Sauce
   Sour cream and shredded Cheddar cheese

For added Cheddar flavor, substitute French's® Cheddar French Fried Onions for the original flavor.

Slow Cooker Directions

1. Cook ground beef, chili powder and cumin in large nonstick skillet over medium heat until browned, stirring frequently; drain. Transfer to slow cooker.

2. Stir in tomatoes with juice, beans, water, *½ cup* French Fried Onions and *Frank's RedHot* Sauce.

3. Cover; cook on LOW setting for 6 hours (or on HIGH for 3 hours). Serve chili topped with sour cream, cheese and remaining onions.   *Makes 8 servings*

Prep Time: 10 minutes
Cook Time: 6 hours

Chili Mole

1 pound ground beef
1 Spanish onion, diced
1 green bell pepper, diced
1 banana pepper, finely chopped
2 jalapeño peppers,* finely chopped
2 cloves garlic, minced
2 cans (about 15 ounces each) kidney beans, rinsed and drained
2 cans (about 14 ounces each) diced tomatoes
1 can (about 4 ounces) tomato paste
1 packet (2 ounces) Cincinnati-style chili seasoning
3 tablespoons unsweetened cocoa powder
2 tablespoons chili powder
1 tablespoon brown sugar
1 tablespoon lime juice

*Jalapeño peppers can sting and irritate the skin, so wear rubber gloves when handling peppers and do not touch your eyes.

1. Brown beef 6 to 8 minutes in Dutch oven over medium-high heat, stirring to separate meat. Drain fat.

2. Add onion and bell pepper; cook and stir until onion is translucent. Add banana pepper, jalapeños and garlic; cook and stir 3 minutes.

3. Stir in beans, tomatoes, tomato paste, chili seasoning, cocoa, chili powder, sugar and lime juice. Cover; simmer 1 hour.   *Makes 6 servings*

tip

If Cincinnati-style chili seasoning is not available, create your own blend. Combine 1 tablespoon chili powder, 1 teaspoon salt, 1 teaspoon black pepper, $\frac{1}{2}$ teaspoon ground allspice, $\frac{1}{2}$ teaspoon ground cinnamon and a pinch of ground cloves.

Smokey Chili with Pasta

2 cups (about 6 ounces) rotelle or rotini pasta, uncooked
1 pound ground beef
1 cup chopped onion
2 cans (about 15 ounces each) red kidney beans
2 cans (10¾ ounces each) condensed tomato soup
2 tablespoons HERSHEY'S Cocoa
2¼ teaspoons chili powder
¾ teaspoon ground black pepper
½ teaspoon salt
Grated Parmesan cheese (optional)

1. Cook pasta according to package directions; drain.

2. Meanwhile, cook ground beef and onion until meat is thoroughly done and onion is tender. If necessary, drain fat.

3. Stir in undrained kidney beans, soup, cocoa, chili powder, pepper and salt. Heat to boiling; reduce heat. Stir in hot pasta; heat thoroughly. Serve with Parmesan cheese, if desired.

Makes 8 servings

Kick'n Chili

2 pounds ground beef
1 tablespoon salt
1 tablespoon cumin
1 tablespoon chili powder
1 tablespoon paprika
1 tablespoon oregano
1 tablespoon black pepper
2 teaspoons red pepper flakes
2 cloves garlic, minced
¼ teaspoon ground red pepper
3 cans (about 10 ounces each) diced tomatoes with green chiles
1 jar (about 16 ounces) salsa
1 onion, chopped

continued on page 158

Kick'n Chili, continued

Slow Cooker Directions

1. Combine beef, salt, cumin, chili powder, paprika, oregano, black pepper, pepper flakes, garlic and ground red pepper in large bowl.

2. Brown beef 6 to 8 minutes in large skillet over medium-high heat, stirring to break up meat. Drain fat. Add tomatoes, salsa and onion; mix well. Transfer beef mixture to slow cooker.

3. Cover; cook on LOW 4 to 6 hours.   *Makes 6 servings*

Variation: This chunky chili is very spicy. Reduce red pepper flakes for a milder flavor.

Red & Green No-Bean Chili

4 pounds ground beef

2 onions, chopped

3 banana peppers, seeded and sliced

¼ cup chili powder

2 tablespoons minced garlic

1 can (about 28 ounces) diced tomatoes with green chiles

1 can (about 14 ounces) beef broth

2 cans (about 4 ounces each) diced mild green chiles, drained

2 tablespoons ground cumin

2 tablespoons cider or malt vinegar

1 to 2 tablespoons ground hot paprika

1 tablespoon dried oregano

  Hot pepper sauce

  Diced avocado and red onions (optional)

1. Brown beef 6 to 8 minutes in large skillet over medium-high heat, stirring to break up meat. Drain fat. Add onions, peppers, chili powder and garlic. Reduce heat to medium-low; cook 30 minutes, stirring occasionally.

2. Add tomatoes, broth, green chiles, cumin, vinegar, paprika, oregano and pepper sauce. Cook 30 minutes, stirring occasionally. Garnish with diced avocado and red onions.

Makes 10 to 12 servings

Slow Cooker Hearty Beef & Bean Chili

1½ **pounds ground beef**

1 **can (10¾ ounces) CAMPBELL'S® Condensed Tomato Soup**
(Regular or Healthy Request®)

½ **cup water**

¼ **cup chili powder**

2 **teaspoons ground cumin**

2 **cloves garlic, minced**

1 **large onion, chopped (about 1 cup)**

2 **cans (about 15 ounces each) red kidney beans, drained**

1 **can (14½ ounces) diced tomatoes**

Slow Cooker Directions

1. Cook the beef in a 10-inch skillet over medium-high heat until the beef is well browned, stirring frequently to separate meat. Pour off any fat. Remove the beef with a slotted spoon and put in a 3½-quart slow cooker.

2. Stir the soup, water, chili powder, cumin, garlic, onion, beans and tomatoes into the cooker.

3. Cover and cook on LOW for 8 to 10 hours.*   *Makes 6 servings*

Or on HIGH for 4 to 5 hours.

Prep Time: 15 minutes
Cook Time: 4 to 10 hours

Cajun Chili

1½ **pounds ground beef**

2 **cans (about 15 ounces each) Cajun-style mixed vegetables**

2 **cans (10¾ ounces each) condensed tomato soup, undiluted**

1 **can (about 14 ounces) diced tomatoes**

3 **sausages with Cheddar cheese (about 8 ounces), cut into bite-size pieces**
Shredded Cheddar cheese (optional)

Slow Cooker Directions

1. Brown beef 6 to 8 minutes in large skillet over medium-high heat, stirring to break up meat. Drain fat.

2. Place beef, mixed vegetables, soup, tomatoes and sausages in slow cooker.

3. Cover; cook on HIGH 2 to 3 hours. Top with cheese.   *Makes 10 servings*

irresistible salads

Chicken and Pasta Salad with Kalamata Olives

- 4 ounces uncooked multigrain rotini pasta
- 2 cups diced cooked chicken
- ½ cup chopped roasted red bell peppers
- 12 pitted kalamata olives, halved
- 1½ tablespoons olive oil
- 1 tablespoon dried basil
- 1 tablespoon cider vinegar
- 1 to 2 cloves garlic, minced
- ¼ teaspoon salt (optional)

1. Cook pasta according to package directions, omitting salt. Drain well; cool.

2. Combine chicken, peppers, olives, oil, basil, vinegar, garlic and salt, if desired, in large bowl.

3. Add cooled pasta to chicken mixture; toss gently.   *Makes 4 servings*

Ravioli Panzanella Salad

1 package (9 ounces) refrigerated cheese ravioli
2 tablespoons olive oil
2 teaspoons white wine vinegar
⅛ teaspoon black pepper
1 cup halved grape tomatoes
½ cup sliced pimiento-stuffed olives
¼ cup finely chopped celery
1 shallot, finely chopped
¼ cup chopped fresh Italian parsley

1. Cook pasta according to package directions. Drain well; transfer to large serving bowl. Let stand 10 minutes.

2. Meanwhile, whisk oil, vinegar and pepper in small bowl until well blended; pour over ravioli. Add tomatoes, olives, celery and shallot; toss gently. Sprinkle with parsley.

Makes 4 servings

tip

Panzanella is a classic Italian salad that pairs a tangy vinaigrette dressing with chopped vegetables and bread cubes. It is a delicious way to use up leftover bread before it goes stale. This salad replaces the bread with ravioli for a tasty variation.

Beef and Pasta Salad with Creamy Blue Cheese Dressing

Creamy Blue Cheese Dressing
- 1/2 **cup mayonnaise**
- 2 **tablespoons crumbled blue cheese**
- 1 **tablespoon white wine vinegar**
- 1/2 **teaspoon dried dill weed**
- 1 **clove garlic, minced**
- 1 **teaspoon lemon juice**

Beef and Pasta Salad
- **Nonstick cooking spray**
- 12 **ounces eye of round steaks or beef tenderloin**
- 8 **ounces radiatore pasta, cooked and cooled**
- 1 1/2 **cups fresh broccoli florets, cooked crisp-tender and cooled**
- 1 **yellow bell pepper, sliced**
- 1 **tomato, cut into wedges**
- 1 **carrot, sliced**
- 1/2 **small red onion, thinly sliced**
- 1/4 **teaspoon salt**
- 1/8 **teaspoon black pepper**

1. For dressing, mix mayonnaise, blue cheese, vinegar, dill weed, garlic and lemon juice in small bowl; refrigerate until ready to use.

2. For salad, spray small skillet with cooking spray; heat over medium heat. Add steaks; cook 7 to 9 minutes or until cooked through (145°F), turning once. Cut beef into 1/4-inch slices.

3. Toss beef, pasta, broccoli, bell pepper, tomato, carrot and onion in large bowl; drizzle with dressing and toss. Season with salt and black pepper.   *Makes 4 servings*

Rotini, Chicken and Spinach Salad

4 cups baby spinach
1½ cups diced cooked chicken breast, chilled
1⅓ cups cooked whole wheat rotini or macaroni
1 tablespoon minced fresh chives
1 teaspoon minced fresh dill
2 tablespoons chicken broth
1 tablespoon olive oil
1½ teaspoons lemon juice
1 teaspoon Dijon mustard
⅛ teaspoon salt
⅛ teaspoon black pepper

1. Combine spinach, chicken, pasta, chives and dill in large bowl; toss gently.

2. Whisk broth, oil, lemon juice, mustard, salt and pepper in small bowl. Pour over salad mixture; toss gently. *Makes 4 servings*

Salmon and Green Bean Salad with Pasta

8 ounces small regular or whole wheat pasta shells
¾ cup fresh green beans, cut into 2-inch pieces
1 can (6 ounces) red salmon, drained and flaked
⅔ cup finely chopped carrots
½ cup cottage cheese
3 tablespoons plain yogurt
1½ tablespoons lemon juice
1 tablespoon chopped fresh dill *or* 1 teaspoon dried dill weed
2 teaspoons grated onion
1 teaspoon Dijon mustard

1. Cook pasta according to package directions; add green beans during last 3 minutes of cooking. Drain; rinse under cold running water until pasta and green beans are cool. Drain well.

2. Combine pasta mixture, salmon and carrots in medium bowl.

3. Place cottage cheese, yogurt, lemon juice, dill, onion and mustard in food processor or blender; process until smooth. Pour over pasta mixture; toss to coat. *Makes 6 servings*

Rotini, Chicken and Spinach Salad

Orange Roughy and Orzo Salad

1½ cups uncooked orzo pasta
¼ cup extra-virgin olive oil
¼ cup sherry vinegar or cider vinegar
2 teaspoons chopped fresh tarragon *or* ½ teaspoon dried tarragon
¼ teaspoon salt
¼ teaspoon white pepper
2 carrots, cut into julienne strips
½ green bell pepper, chopped
⅓ cup cornmeal
1 tablespoon Cajun seasoning
¾ pound orange roughy fillets
  Vegetable oil
1 cup chopped fresh parsley

1. Cook orzo according to package directions. Drain; place in large bowl.

2. Combine olive oil, vinegar, tarragon, salt and white pepper in small bowl; toss with orzo. Top with carrots and bell pepper; refrigerate.

3. Mix cornmeal and Cajun seasoning in shallow dish. Rinse orange roughy and pat dry with paper towels. Cut into 2×1-inch strips. Coat with cornmeal mixture.

4. Pour enough vegetable oil into large skillet to coat bottom; heat over medium-high heat. Add half of fish strips; cook 4 minutes or until golden brown, turning once. Remove cooked fish and drain on paper towels. Repeat with remaining fish.

5. To serve, toss orzo mixture with chopped parsley. Transfer to serving platter. Arrange warm fish strips over top of salad.

Makes 4 servings

Thai Chicken Fettuccine Salad

 6 ounces uncooked fettuccine
 1 cup salsa, plus additional for serving
 1/4 cup chunky peanut butter
 2 tablespoons orange juice
 2 tablespoons honey
 1 teaspoon soy sauce
 1/2 teaspoon ground ginger
 2 tablespoons vegetable oil
 3 boneless skinless chicken breasts (about 1 pound), cut into 1-inch pieces
  Lettuce or savoy cabbage leaves (optional)
 1/4 cup coarsely chopped fresh cilantro
 1/4 cup peanuts
 1/4 cup thin red bell pepper strips, cut into halves

1. Cook pasta according to package directions; drain.

2. Meanwhile, combine salsa, peanut butter, orange juice, honey, soy sauce and ginger in small saucepan. Cook and stir over low heat until blended and smooth. Reserve 1/4 cup salsa mixture.

3. Place pasta in large bowl. Pour remaining salsa mixture over pasta; toss gently to coat.

4. Heat oil in large skillet over medium-high heat. Cook and stir chicken about 5 minutes or until cooked through. Add reserved 1/4 cup salsa mixture; mix well.

5. Arrange pasta on lettuce-lined platter, if desired. Place chicken mixture on pasta. Top with cilantro, peanuts and pepper strips.

6. Refrigerate until mixture is cooled to room temperature. Serve with additional salsa.

Makes 4 servings

Couscous Turkey Salad

Salad

    1 cup plus 2 tablespoons chicken broth
    ¼ teaspoon salt
    ¾ cup uncooked Israeli or pearl couscous
    1½ cups chopped cooked turkey
    1 cup shredded carrots
    1 stalk celery, trimmed and finely chopped
    1 green onion, trimmed and chopped
    2 tablespoons toasted pine nuts*
        Salad greens (optional)

Dressing

    2 tablespoons jellied cranberry sauce
    2 tablespoons vegetable oil
    4 teaspoons balsamic vinegar
    ½ teaspoon curry powder
    ¼ teaspoon salt
    ¼ teaspoon black pepper

To toast pine nuts, place in small skillet over medium-high heat about 2 minutes or until fragrant, stirring constantly.

1. For salad, combine broth and salt in small saucepan; bring to a boil. Stir in couscous; cover and reduce heat to low. Simmer 3 to 5 minutes or until liquid is absorbed and couscous is tender. Remove from heat; chill.

2. Meanwhile, combine turkey, carrots, celery, green onion and nuts in large bowl. Stir in couscous.

3. For dressing, stir together cranberry sauce, oil, vinegar, curry powder, salt and pepper in small bowl. Pour over salad; toss well. Serve on bed of salad greens, if desired.

Makes 4 servings

tip

Israeli couscous, also called pearl couscous, is the size of small pearls and cooks like pasta. If you can't find Israeli or pearl couscous in your supermarket, use plain packaged couscous. Prepare couscous as directed on package, using the amount of chicken broth and salt called for in the recipe.

Thai Chicken Broccoli Salad

    4 ounces uncooked linguine
      Nonstick cooking spray
½ pound boneless skinless chicken breasts, cut into bite-size pieces
    2 cups broccoli florets
    2 tablespoons cold water
⅔ cup chopped red bell pepper
    6 green onions, sliced diagonally into 1-inch pieces
¼ cup creamy peanut butter
    2 tablespoons *each* hot water and soy sauce
    2 teaspoons dark sesame oil
½ teaspoon red pepper flakes
⅛ teaspoon garlic powder
¼ cup unsalted peanuts, chopped

1. Cook pasta according to package directions, omitting salt. Drain.

2. Spray large nonstick skillet with cooking spray; heat over medium-high heat. Add chicken; cook and stir 5 minutes or until chicken is cooked through. Transfer to large bowl.

3. Add broccoli and cold water to skillet. Cook covered, 2 minutes. Uncover; cook and stir 2 minutes or until broccoli is crisp-tender. Transfer broccoli to bowl; add pasta, bell pepper and green onions.

4. Combine peanut butter, hot water, soy sauce, oil, pepper flakes and garlic powder in small bowl until well blended. Drizzle over pasta mixture; toss to coat. Top with peanuts before serving.
Makes 4 servings

Roast Beef and Pasta Salad

    9 ounces uncooked radiatore pasta
    6 ounces roast beef
    1 can (about 15 ounces) kidney beans, rinsed and drained
    1 can (15 ounces) whole baby corn, rinsed and drained
    1 can (10 ounces) diced tomatoes and green chiles
    1 cup cherry tomato halves
¼ cup olive oil
    2 tablespoons minced fresh parsley
    1 tablespoon minced fresh oregano

continued on page 174

Thai Chicken Broccoli Salad

Roast Beef and Pasta Salad, continued

1. Cook pasta according to package directions, omitting salt. Drain. Rinse in cold water and drain.

2. Slice beef into thin strips. Combine pasta, beef, beans, corn, diced tomatoes, cherry tomatoes, oil, parsley and oregano in large bowl. Toss to coat.   *Makes 6 servings*

Prep and Cook Time: 25 minutes

Fettuccine Niçoise Salad

   8 ounces green beans, cut into 2-inch pieces
   1 package (9 ounces) fresh fettuccine
½ cup coarsely chopped pitted niçoise or kalamata olives
   2 tomatoes, cored and chopped
   1 can or package (6 ounces) tuna packed in water, drained and flaked
¼ cup olive oil
   1 tablespoon white wine vinegar or fresh lemon juice
¼ teaspoon salt
¼ teaspoon black pepper
¼ cup finely chopped fresh basil

1. Bring large saucepan of salted water to a boil. Add green beans; cook 2 to 5 minutes or until bright green and crisp-tender. Remove beans from water; drain well.

2. Bring water back to a boil. Add pasta; cook according to package directions. Drain well. Arrange green beans, pasta, olives, tomatoes and tuna on plates.

3. Combine oil, vinegar, salt and pepper in small bowl; pour over salad. Sprinkle with basil.
                                        Makes 4 servings

Cajun Pork with Pasta Salad

    Cajun Spice Rub (recipe follows)
1 **boneless pork tenderloin (about 12 ounces), cut into ¼-inch-thick slices**
    Nonstick cooking spray
8 **ounces sliced okra**
½ *each* **red and yellow bell peppers, sliced**
1 **teaspoon minced jalapeño pepper***
1 **onion, sliced**
¼ **cup chicken broth**
    Salt and black pepper
8 **ounces bow tie pasta, cooked and kept warm**

*Jalapeño peppers can sting and irritate the skin, so wear rubber gloves when handling peppers and do not touch your eyes.

1. Prepare Cajun Spice Rub; coat all sides of pork.

2. Spray large skillet with cooking spray; heat over medium heat. Cook and stir pork 2 to 3 minutes on each side until browned and no longer pink in center. Remove from skillet; set aside.

3. Add okra to skillet; cook 3 to 5 minutes or until browned. Add bell peppers, jalapeño, onion and broth; bring to a boil. Reduce heat and simmer covered, 3 to 5 minutes or until vegetables are crisp-tender. Add pork; cook 2 to 3 minutes. Season to taste with salt and black pepper.

4. Toss pasta with pork mixture.   *Makes 4 servings*

Cajun Spice Rub

2 **teaspoons dried oregano**
1 **teaspoon** *each* **garlic powder and dried thyme**
½ **teaspoon** *each* **dry mustard and paprika**
¼ **teaspoon** *each* **salt, dried cumin, ground allspice, ground red pepper and black pepper**

1. Combine oregano, thyme, garlic powder, paprika, dry mustard, salt, cumin, allspice, red pepper and black pepper in small bowl.   *Makes about 2 tablespoons*

mac &
cheese

Mac and Cheese Toss

8 ounces ham, diced
4 cups (1 quart) prepared macaroni and cheese
½ cup frozen green peas, thawed
¼ cup milk

1. Combine ham, macaroni and cheese, peas and milk in microwavable 2-quart casserole. Toss gently to blend.

2. Microwave covered, on HIGH 3 minutes; stir. Microwave 1 minute or until heated through.

Makes 4 servings

7 Veggie Mac 'n Cheese

1 can (15 ounces) VEG•ALL® Original Mixed Vegetables, drained
1 box (7¼ ounces) macaroni and cheese mix, prepared
1 teaspoon onion powder
1 teaspoon prepared mustard
1 tomato, sliced
1 teaspoon dried parsley

Preheat oven to 350°F. Combine Veg•All, prepared macaroni and cheese, onion powder, and mustard; mix well. Pour into greased 1-quart casserole. Bake for 20 to 25 minutes. Garnish with tomato slices and dried parsley. Serve hot.

Makes 6 servings

Prep Time: 7 minutes
Cook Time: 20 minutes

My Mac & Cheese

¼ cup (½ stick) butter

¼ cup all-purpose flour

2 cups milk

2 cups (8 ounces) shredded sharp Cheddar cheese

½ cup (2 ounces) shredded Monterey Jack cheese (optional)

½ cup chopped onion

2 cups (about 16 ounces) broccoli florets, steamed

2 cups elbow macaroni, cooked and drained

2 English muffins, cut into ½-inch pieces

1. Preheat oven to 350°F.

2. Melt butter in large saucepan over medium heat. Stir in flour until smooth; cook and stir 2 minutes. Gradually add milk, stirring constantly, until mixture is slightly thickened.

3. Add Cheddar, Monterey Jack, if desired, and onion. Cook and stir until cheese melts. Add broccoli; stir well.

4. Place macaroni in 3-quart casserole. Add cheese mixture; mix well. Sprinkle English muffin pieces evenly over top. Bake 15 to 20 minutes or until muffin pieces are golden brown.

Makes 4 to 6 servings

Crispy Macaroni & Cheese

1 can (10¾ ounces) CAMPBELL'S® Condensed Cream of Mushroom Soup or 98% Fat Free Cream of Mushroom Soup

½ cup milk

½ teaspoon prepared mustard

Generous dash pepper

2 cups shredded Cheddar cheese (8 ounces)

3 cups hot cooked elbow macaroni (about 1½ cups uncooked)

1 can (2.8 ounces) French fried onions (1⅓ cups)

1. In 1½-quart casserole mix soup, milk, mustard, pepper, *1½ **cups cheese*** and macaroni. Bake at 400°F. for 20 minutes or until hot.

2. Stir. Sprinkle French fried onions and remaining cheese over top. Bake 1 minute more or until onions are golden.

Makes 4 servings

Prep Time: 20 minutes
Cook Time: 20 minutes

Easy Cheese & Tomato Macaroni

2 packages (7 ounces each) macaroni and cheese dinner
1 tablespoon olive or vegetable oil
1 cup finely chopped onion
1 cup thinly sliced celery
1 can (28 ounces) CONTADINA® Recipe Ready Original Crushed Tomatoes
  Grated Parmesan cheese (optional)
  Sliced green onion or celery leaves (optional)

1. Cook macaroni (from macaroni and cheese dinner) according to package directions; drain.

2. Heat oil in large skillet. Add chopped onion and celery; sauté for 3 minutes or until vegetables are tender.

3. Combine tomatoes and cheese mixes from dinners in small bowl. Stir into vegetable mixture.

4. Simmer for 3 to 4 minutes or until mixture is thickened and heated through. Add macaroni to skillet; stir until well coated with sauce. Heat thoroughly, stirring occasionally. Sprinkle with Parmesan cheese and sliced green onion, if desired. *Makes 6 to 8 servings*

Prep Time: 5 minutes
Cook Time: 15 minutes

Four-Cheese Mac & Cheese

1 package (16 ounces) uncooked elbow macaroni
4 cups milk
4 cups (16 ounces) shredded sharp Cheddar cheese
4 cups (16 ounces) shredded American cheese
2 cups (8 ounces) shredded Muenster cheese
2 cups (8 ounces) shredded mozzarella cheese
½ cup dry bread crumbs (optional)

1. Preheat oven to 350°F. Cook macaroni according to package directions. Drain; keep warm.

2. Bring milk to a simmer in large saucepan over medium heat. Reduce heat to low. Gradually add cheeses, stirring constantly. Cook and stir 5 minutes or until smooth.

3. Place macaroni in 4-quart casserole or individual ovenproof dishes. Pour cheese sauce over macaroni; stir until well blended. Sprinkle with bread crumbs, if desired. Bake 50 to 60 minutes or until bubbly and heated through. *Makes 8 servings*

Easy Cheese & Tomato Macaroni

Old-Fashioned Macaroni & Cheese with Broccoli

2 cups (8 ounces) uncooked elbow macaroni

3 cups small broccoli florets

1 tablespoon butter

1 tablespoon all-purpose flour

¹⁄₂ teaspoon salt

¹⁄₈ teaspoon black pepper

1³⁄₄ cups milk

1¹⁄₂ cups shredded sharp Cheddar cheese

1. Cook macaroni according to package directions, omitting salt. Add broccoli during last 5 minutes of cooking time. Drain pasta and broccoli; return to pan.

2. Meanwhile, melt butter in small saucepan over medium heat. Add flour, salt and pepper; cook and stir 1 minute. Stir in milk; bring to a boil over medium-high heat, stirring frequently. Reduce heat and simmer 2 minutes. Remove from heat. Gradually stir in cheese until melted.

3. Add sauce to macaroni and broccoli; stir until blended. *Makes 8 servings*

Velveeta® Ultimate Macaroni & Cheese

2 cups (8 ounces) elbow macaroni, uncooked

³⁄₄ pound (12 ounces) VELVEETA® Pasteurized Prepared Cheese Product, cut into ¹⁄₂-inch cubes

¹⁄₃ cup milk

¹⁄₈ teaspoon black pepper

Cook macaroni as directed on package; drain well. Return to pan.

Add remaining ingredients; mix well. Cook on low heat until VELVEETA® is completely melted and mixture is well blended, stirring frequently. *Makes 4 servings, 1 cup each*

Prep Time: 20 minutes
Total Time: 20 minutes

Variation: Prepare as directed. Pour into 2-quart casserole dish. Bake at 350°F for 25 minutes.

Dressed-up Mac 'n Cheese: Substitute bow tie pasta or your favorite shaped pasta for the macaroni.

Pesto Chicken Mac & Cheese

4 cups milk
1 clove garlic, crushed
¼ cup (½ stick) butter
5 tablespoons all-purpose flour
8 ounces fontina cheese, shredded
2 cups (8 ounces) shredded mozzarella cheese
½ cup grated Parmesan cheese
½ cup pesto
    Salt and black pepper
1 package (16 ounces) radiatore or penne pasta, cooked and drained
1 pound boneless skinless chicken breasts, cooked and chopped
1 package (6 ounces) baby spinach

1. Bring milk and garlic to a boil in small saucepan. Remove from heat; discard garlic.

2. Melt butter in large saucepan over medium heat; whisk in flour. Cook and stir 2 minutes. Gradually add warm milk, whisking constantly until smooth. Bring to a boil. Reduce heat; cook and stir 10 minutes or until thickened. Remove from heat.

3. Add cheeses to sauce, whisking until smooth. Stir in pesto; season with salt and pepper. Toss pasta, chicken and spinach with pesto mixture until spinach wilts. Serve immediately.

Makes 6 to 8 servings

Ranchero Macaroni Bake

1 can (26 ounces) CAMPBELL'S® Condensed Cream of Mushroom Soup
    or 98% Fat Free Cream of Mushroom Soup
1 cup milk
1 cup PACE® Chunky Salsa or Picante Sauce
3 cups shredded Cheddar or Monterey Jack cheese (12 ounces)
6 cups hot cooked elbow macaroni (about 3 cups uncooked)
1 cup coarsely crushed tortilla chips

1. Mix soup, milk, salsa, cheese and macaroni. Spoon into 3-quart shallow baking dish.

2. Bake at 400°F. for 20 minutes or until hot.

3. Stir. Sprinkle chips over macaroni mixture. Bake 5 minutes more.

Makes 8 servings

Prep Time: 20 minutes
Cook Time: 25 minutes

Stovetop Macaroni and Cheese

  1 tablespoon salt
12 ounces elbow macaroni, uncooked
  1 (12-ounce) can evaporated milk
¼ cup CREAM OF WHEAT® Hot Cereal (Instant, 1-minute, 2½-minute
    or 10-minute cook time), uncooked
  2 eggs
  1 teaspoon Dijon mustard
½ teaspoon TRAPPEY'S® Red Devil™ Cayenne Pepper Sauce
½ teaspoon salt
  8 ounces Cheddar cheese, shredded
½ cup milk

1. Bring large pot of water to a boil. Stir in salt. Add macaroni. Stir, then cook 8 minutes or until tender. Drain and return pasta to pot.

2. While pasta is cooking, whisk evaporated milk, Cream of Wheat, eggs, mustard, pepper sauce and salt in medium bowl.

3. Add mixture to cooked pasta. Cook and stir over medium-low heat until mixture thickens. Gradually stir in cheese, adding more as it melts. Add ½ cup milk; stir until creamy. Serve warm. *Makes 6 servings*

Prep Time: 5 minutes
Start to Finish Time: 20 minutes

tip

For a nice garnish and extra crunch, combine ¼ cup fresh bread crumbs with ¼ cup Cream of Wheat. Melt 1 tablespoon butter in small saucepan over medium heat. Add Cream of Wheat mixture; cook and stir until mixture is golden brown. Sprinkle on top of each serving.

Traditional Macaroni & Cheese

  2 tablespoons cornstarch
  1 teaspoon salt
  ½ teaspoon dry mustard
  ¼ teaspoon ground black pepper
  1 can (12 fluid ounces) NESTLÉ® CARNATION® Evaporated Milk
  1 cup water
  2 tablespoons butter or margarine
  2 cups (8 ounces) shredded sharp Cheddar cheese, divided
1⅔ cups (about 7 ounces) dry small elbow macaroni, cooked and drained

PREHEAT oven to 375°F. Grease 2-quart casserole dish.

COMBINE cornstarch, salt, mustard and pepper in medium saucepan. Stir in evaporated milk, water and butter. Cook over medium heat, stirring constantly, until mixture comes to a boil. Boil for 1 minute. Remove from heat. Stir in *1½ cups* cheese until melted. Add macaroni; mix well. Pour into prepared casserole dish. Top with remaining cheese.

BAKE for 20 to 25 minutes or until cheese is melted and light brown.   *Makes 6 servings*

Note: To transform Macaroni & Cheese from a simple dish to a savory one-dish meal, add 1 cup chopped ham or hot dogs after milk mixture comes to a boil.

Zesty Macaroni & Cheese

1½ cups uncooked elbow macaroni
  1 can (10¾ ounces) condensed cream of mushroom soup, undiluted
  2 cups shredded Cheddar cheese
  ½ cup milk
  2 teaspoons minced onion
  2 teaspoons diced green bell pepper
  2 teaspoons creamy horseradish sauce
  ½ teaspoon dry mustard
  ½ teaspoon ground white pepper
  ½ teaspoon salt
  3 slices sharp Cheddar cheese

1. Preheat oven to 375°F. Spray 2-quart baking dish with nonstick cooking spray. Cook macaroni according to package directions. Drain. Combine soup, shredded cheese, milk, onion, bell pepper, horseradish sauce, mustard, white pepper and salt in large bowl; mix well. Add macaroni; mix well.

2. Place macaroni mixture in prepared dish. Top with cheese slices; cover and bake 30 minutes or until heated through.   *Makes 6 servings*

Italian Three-Cheese Macaroni

2 cups uncooked elbow macaroni
¼ cup (½ stick) butter
3 tablespoons all-purpose flour
1 teaspoon Italian seasoning
½ to 1 teaspoon black pepper
½ teaspoon salt
2 cups milk
¾ cup (3 ounces) shredded Cheddar cheese
¼ cup grated Parmesan cheese
1 can (about 14 ounces) diced tomatoes, drained
1 cup (4 ounces) shredded mozzarella cheese
½ cup dry bread crumbs

1. Preheat oven to 350°F. Spray 2-quart round casserole with nonstick cooking spray.

2. Cook macaroni according to package directions until al dente. Drain and set aside.

3. Melt butter in medium saucepan over medium heat. Whisk in flour, Italian seasoning, pepper and salt, stirring until smooth. Gradually add milk, whisking constantly until slightly thickened. Add Cheddar and Parmesan; stir until smooth.

4. Layer half of pasta, half of tomatoes and half of cheese sauce in prepared dish. Repeat layers.

5. Sprinkle mozzarella and bread crumbs evenly over casserole.

6. Bake covered, 30 minutes or until bubbly and heated through. Uncover and bake 5 minutes or until top is golden brown. *Makes 4 servings*

Salsa Macaroni & Cheese

1 jar (1 pound) RAGÚ® Cheesy! Double Cheddar Sauce
1 cup prepared mild salsa
8 ounces elbow macaroni, cooked and drained

1. In 2-quart saucepan, heat Double Cheddar Sauce over medium heat. Stir in salsa; heat through.

2. Toss with hot macaroni. Serve immediately. *Makes 4 servings*

Prep Time: 5 minutes
Cook Time: 15 minutes

Enlightened Macaroni and Cheese

8 ounces uncooked rotini pasta or elbow macaroni
1 tablespoon all-purpose flour
2 teaspoons cornstarch
¼ teaspoon dry mustard
1 can (12 ounces) evaporated milk
1 cup (4 ounces) shredded sharp Cheddar cheese
½ cup (2 ounces) shredded Monterey Jack cheese
1 jar (2 ounces) diced pimiento, drained and rinsed
1 teaspoon Worcestershire sauce
¼ teaspoon black pepper
1 tablespoon plain dry bread crumbs
1 tablespoon paprika

1. Preheat oven to 375°F.

2. Cook macaroni according to package directions, omitting salt. Drain and set aside.

3. Combine flour, cornstarch and mustard in medium saucepan; stir in evaporated milk until smooth. Cook and stir over low heat about 8 minutes or until slightly thickened.

4. Remove from heat; stir in cheeses, pimiento, Worcestershire and pepper. Add pasta; mix well.

5. Spray 1½-quart casserole with nonstick cooking spray. Spoon mixture into casserole; sprinkle with bread crumbs and paprika.

6. Bake 20 minutes or until bubbly and heated through. *Makes 6 servings*

South-of-the-Border Mac and Cheese

1 package (7.25 ounces each) macaroni and cheese dinner
1 pound ground sirloin beef
1 can (10 ounces each) RO*TEL® Original Diced Tomatoes & Green Chilies, undrained
1 cup shredded Cheddar cheese (optional)

1. Prepare macaroni and cheese in large saucepan according to package directions, except omit milk.

2. Brown beef in a large skillet over medium-high heat while macaroni cooks; drain. Add undrained tomatoes; mix well. Reduce heat to low; simmer 5 minutes, stirring occasionally.

3. Add beef mixture to prepared macaroni and cheese; sprinkle with Cheddar cheese, if desired.   *Makes 5 servings*

Cook Time: 15 minutes
Total Time: 25 minutes

Macaroni and Cheese with Mixed Vegetables

1¼ cups milk, divided
2 tablespoons all-purpose flour
½ cup shredded sharp Cheddar cheese
½ cup shredded Parmesan cheese
1½ cups frozen mixed vegetables, cooked and drained
1⅓ cups cooked elbow macaroni, rotini or penne
¼ teaspoon salt
⅛ teaspoon black pepper

1. Preheat oven to 325°F. Coat 1½-quart baking dish with nonstick cooking spray; set aside.

2. Stir ¼ cup milk and flour in small bowl until smooth. Add remaining 1 cup milk; stir until well blended. Pour into small saucepan. Bring mixture to a simmer over medium heat, stirring constantly, until thickened.

3. Combine cheeses in separate medium bowl. Stir half of cheese mixture into saucepan. Reserve remaining cheese mixture. Add vegetables, macaroni, salt and pepper to saucepan.

4. Spoon macaroni mixture into prepared baking dish. Sprinkle with reserved cheese mixture. Bake 20 minutes or until cheese melts and macaroni is heated through. Remove from oven. Let stand 5 minutes before serving.   *Makes 4 servings*

Southern Macaroni and Cheese

1½ cups cooked whole wheat or multigrain elbow macaroni
2 teaspoons all-purpose flour
1 tablespoon dry mustard
½ teaspoon salt
½ teaspoon black pepper
1 cup milk, divided
½ cup plus 1 tablespoon shredded sharp Cheddar cheese, divided
1 egg white
1 tablespoon unseasoned dry bread crumbs
⅛ teaspoon paprika

1. Preheat oven to 325°F. Spray 1-quart baking dish with nonstick cooking spray.

2. Cook macaroni according to package directions. Drain. Rinse under cold water to cool slightly. Drain and set aside.

3. Combine flour, mustard, salt and pepper in small saucepan; whisk in ½ cup milk. Place over medium heat; stir in remaining ½ cup milk. Cook and stir until bubbly and thickened. Remove from heat; let cool 2 to 3 minutes. Stir in ½ cup cheese until melted.

4. Stir egg white into macaroni. Stir in cheese sauce. Spoon macaroni mixture into prepared dish.

5. Combine remaining 1 tablespoon cheese, bread crumbs and paprika; sprinkle mixture over macaroni. Bake 15 to 20 minutes or until bubbly and lightly browned. Let stand 5 minutes before serving.
Makes 4 servings

No Boiling Mexicali Mac & Cheese Bake

1 jar (1 pound) RAGÚ® Cheesy! Double Cheddar Sauce
1½ cups water
1 can (4 ounces) diced green chilies, undrained
1 cup chopped fresh tomatoes
1 cup (about 4 ounces) shredded Monterey Jack cheese, divided
8 ounces uncooked elbow macaroni

continued on page 196

No Boiling Mexicali Mac & Cheese Bake, continued

1. Preheat oven to 400°F.

2. In large bowl, combine Double Cheddar Sauce, water, chilies, tomatoes and ¹/₂ cup cheese. Stir in uncooked macaroni.

3. In 2-quart casserole, spoon macaroni mixture, then cover tightly with aluminum foil. Bake 45 minutes. Remove foil and sprinkle with remaining ¹/₂ cup cheese. Bake, uncovered, an additional 5 minutes. Let stand 5 minutes before serving.   *Makes 8 servings*

Prep Time: 5 minutes
Cook Time: 50 minutes

Baked Macaroni & Cheese

1 can (10¾ ounces) CAMPBELL'S® Condensed Cheddar Cheese Soup
¹/₂ soup can milk
¹/₈ teaspoon ground black pepper
2 cups hot cooked corkscrew or medium shell macaroni
    (about 1¹/₂ cups uncooked)
1 tablespoon dry bread crumbs
2 teaspoons butter, melted

1. Stir the soup, milk, black pepper and pasta in a 1-quart casserole.

2. Mix the bread crumbs with the butter in a small bowl. Sprinkle over the pasta mixture.

3. Bake at 400°F. for 20 minutes or until hot.   *Makes 4 servings*

Prep Time: 20 minutes
Cook Time: 20 minutes

To Double Recipe: Double all ingredients, except increase butter to 1 tablespoon, use 2-quart casserole and increase baking time to 25 minutes.

Variation: Substitute 2 cups hot cooked elbow macaroni (about 1 cup uncooked) for corkscrew *or* shell macaroni.

Velveeta® Down-Home Macaroni & Cheese

¼ cup (½ stick) butter or margarine, divided
¼ cup all-purpose flour
1 cup milk
½ pound (8 ounces) VELVEETA® Pasteurized Prepared Cheese Product,
  cut into ½-inch cubes
2 cups elbow macaroni, cooked, drained
½ cup KRAFT® Shredded Cheddar Cheese
¼ cup crushed RITZ® Crackers

Preheat oven to 350°F. Melt 3 tablespoons of the butter in medium saucepan over low heat. Add flour; mix well. Cook 2 minutes, stirring constantly. Gradually add milk, stirring until well blended. Cook over medium heat until mixture boils and thickens, stirring constantly. Add VELVEETA®; cook until melted, stirring frequently. Add macaroni; mix lightly.

Spoon into lightly greased 2-quart casserole dish; sprinkle with shredded cheese. Melt remaining 1 tablespoon butter; toss with cracker crumbs. Sprinkle over casserole.

Bake 20 minutes or until heated through.   *Makes 5 servings*

Prep Time: 20 minutes
Total Time: 40 minutes

Jazz It Up: Stir in ¼ cup OSCAR MAYER® Real Bacon Bits with the cooked macaroni.

hearty
soups

Italian Sausage Soup

Sausage Meatballs

    1 pound Italian sausage, casings removed

    ½ cup plain dry bread crumbs

    ¼ cup grated Parmesan cheese

    ¼ cup milk

    1 egg

    ½ teaspoon *each* dried basil and black pepper

    ¼ teaspoon garlic salt

Soup

    4 cups chicken broth

    1 tablespoon tomato paste

    1 clove garlic, minced

    ¼ teaspoon red pepper flakes

    ½ cup uncooked miniature shell pasta*

    1 bag (10 ounces) baby spinach

    Additional grated Parmesan cheese (optional)

Or use other tiny pasta, such as ditalini (mini tubes) or farfallini (mini bow ties).

Slow Cooker Directions

1. Combine all meatball ingredients in large bowl. Shape into marble-size balls.

2. Combine broth, tomato paste, garlic and pepper flakes in slow cooker. Add meatballs. Cover; cook on LOW 5 to 6 hours.

3. Add pasta; cook on LOW 30 minutes or until pasta is tender. Stir in spinach until wilted. Ladle into bowls; sprinkle with cheese, if desired. Serve immediately.   *Makes 4 to 6 servings*

Asian Pasta & Shrimp Soup

1 package (3½ ounces) fresh shiitake mushrooms

2 teaspoons Asian sesame oil

2 cans (14½ ounces each) vegetable broth

4 ounces angel hair pasta, broken into 2-inch lengths (about 1 cup)

½ pound medium shrimp, peeled and deveined

4 ounces snow peas, cut into thin strips

2 tablespoons *French's*® Honey Dijon Mustard

1 tablespoon *Frank's*® *RedHot*® Original Cayenne Pepper Sauce

⅛ teaspoon ground ginger

1. Remove and discard stems from mushrooms. Cut mushrooms into thin strips. Heat oil in large saucepan over medium-high heat. Add mushrooms; stir-fry 3 minutes or just until tender.

2. Add broth and *½ cup water* to saucepan. Heat to boiling. Stir in pasta. Cook 2 minutes or just until tender.

3. Add remaining ingredients, stirring frequently. Heat to boiling. Reduce heat to medium-low. Cook 2 minutes or until shrimp turn pink and peas are tender.   *Makes 4 servings*

Prep Time: 10 minutes
Cook Time: about 10 minutes

Sensational Chicken Noodle Soup

4 cups SWANSON® Chicken Broth (Regular, Natural Goodness® or Certified Organic)
Generous dash ground black pepper
1 medium carrot, sliced (about ½ cup)
1 stalk celery, sliced (about ½ cup)
½ cup uncooked medium egg noodles
1 cup cubed cooked chicken or turkey

1. Heat the broth, black pepper, carrot and celery in a 2-quart saucepan over medium-high heat to a boil.

2. Stir in the noodles and chicken. Reduce the heat to medium. Cook for 10 minutes or until the noodles are tender but still firm. *Makes 4 servings*

Prep Time: 5 minutes
Cook Time: 20 minutes

Quick & Easy Ravioli Soup

½ pound Italian sausage, casings removed
½ cup chopped onion
1 clove garlic, crushed
2 cans (about 14 ounces each) chicken broth
2 cups water
1 package (9 ounces) frozen mini cheese-filled ravioli
1 can (about 15 ounces) garbanzo beans, rinsed and drained
1 can (about 14 ounces) diced tomatoes with green chiles
¾ teaspoon dried oregano
½ teaspoon black pepper
1 cup fresh baby spinach
Grated Parmesan cheese

1. Cook sausage, onion and garlic 5 minutes in Dutch oven over medium heat, stirring to break up meat. Drain fat. Remove sausage mixture; set aside.

2. Add broth and water to Dutch oven; bring to a boil over medium-high heat. Add pasta; cook 4 to 5 minutes or until tender. Stir in sausage mixture, beans, tomatoes, oregano and pepper; heat through. Stir in spinach; cook about 1 minute or until wilted. Ladle into bowls. Sprinkle evenly with cheese. *Makes 8 servings*

Sensational Chicken Noodle Soup

Rich and Hearty Drumstick Soup

4 cups chicken broth

3 cups water

2 turkey drumsticks (about 1¾ pounds)

3 carrots, peeled and sliced

3 stalks celery, thinly sliced

1 onion, chopped

2 cloves garlic, minced

1 teaspoon poultry seasoning

8 ounces uncooked egg noodles

⅓ cup chopped parsley

Slow Cooker Directions

1. Combine broth, water, drumsticks, carrots, celery, onion, garlic and poultry seasoning in slow cooker. Cover; cook on HIGH 5 hours or until meat is falling off bones. Remove turkey; set aside. Add noodles; cover and cook 30 minutes or until noodles are tender.

2. Meanwhile, remove and discard skin and bones from turkey; shred meat. Return to slow cooker. Cover; cook until heated through. Stir in parsley. Season with salt and pepper.

Makes 8 servings

Asian Noodle Soup

4 ounces uncooked dried Chinese egg noodles

3 cans (about 14 ounces each) chicken broth

2 slices fresh ginger

2 cloves garlic, cut into halves

½ cup fresh snow peas, cut into 1-inch pieces

3 tablespoons chopped green onions

1 tablespoon chopped fresh cilantro

1½ teaspoons hot chili oil

½ teaspoon dark sesame oil

1. Cook noodles according to package directions, omitting salt. Drain and set aside.

2. Combine broth, ginger and garlic in large saucepan; bring to a boil over high heat. Reduce heat to low; simmer about 15 minutes. Remove and discard ginger and garlic.

3. Add snow peas, green onions, cilantro, chili oil and sesame oil to broth; simmer 3 to 5 minutes. Stir in noodles; heat through. Serve immediately.

Makes 4 servings

Rich and Hearty Drumstick Soup

Chicken Tortellini Soup

2 tablespoons olive oil

4 boneless, skinless chicken breast halves, cut into bite-size pieces

2 ribs celery, cut into ¼-inch slices

1 medium carrot, cut into ¼-inch slices

1 medium onion, diced

2 cloves garlic, minced

6 cups canned or packaged fat free, reduced sodium chicken broth

2 cups water

1 can (14½ ounces) diced tomatoes

2 small zucchini, halved lengthwise, cut in ½-inch slices

½ teaspoon pepper

½ teaspoon Italian seasoning

1 package (9 ounces) plain or spinach cheese-filled tortellini

Salt to taste

Freshly grated Parmesan cheese

In 5-quart saucepan or Dutch oven, place oil and heat to medium high temperature. Add chicken, celery, carrot, onion and garlic; cook, stirring, about 8 minutes or until chicken is lightly browned and vegetables are tender-crisp. Add broth, water, tomatoes, zucchini, pepper and Italian seasoning. Heat to boiling; reduce heat, cover and cook 7 minutes. Return to boiling, add tortellini and cook 7 minutes or until tortellini are done. Serve in individual bowls; top with a sprinkle of Parmesan cheese.   *Makes 6 servings*

Favorite recipe from **Delmarva Poultry Industry, Inc.**

Spicy Lentil and Pasta Soup

    Nonstick cooking spray
  2 **onions, thinly sliced**
½ **cup chopped carrot**
½ **cup chopped celery**
½ **cup peeled and chopped turnip**
  1 **jalapeño pepper,* finely chopped**
  2 **cups water**
  2 **cans (about 14 ounces each) vegetable broth**
  1 **can (about 14 ounces) stewed tomatoes**
  8 **ounces dried lentils, sorted, rinsed and drained**
  2 **teaspoons chili powder**
½ **teaspoon dried oregano**
  3 **ounces uncooked spaghetti, broken**
¼ **cup minced fresh cilantro**

*Jalapeño peppers can sting and irritate the skin, so wear rubber gloves when handling peppers and do not touch your eyes.

1. Spray large nonstick saucepan with cooking spray; heat over medium heat. Add onions, carrot, celery, turnip and jalapeño; cook and stir 10 minutes or until vegetables are crisp-tender.

2. Add water, broth, tomatoes, lentils, chili powder and oregano; bring to a boil. Reduce heat; simmer covered, 20 to 30 minutes or until lentils are tender.

3. Add pasta; cook 10 minutes or until tender. Ladle soup into bowls; sprinkle with cilantro.

Makes 6 servings

Hearty Minestrone Soup

  2 **cans (10¾ ounces each) condensed Italian tomato soup**
  3 **cups water**
  3 **cups cooked vegetables, such as zucchini, peas, corn or beans**
  2 **cups cooked ditalini pasta**
1⅓ **cups *French's*® French Fried Onions**

1. Combine soup and water in large saucepan. Add vegetables and pasta. Bring to a boil. Reduce heat. Cook until heated through, stirring often.

2. Place French Fried Onions in microwavable dish. Microwave on HIGH 1 minute or until onions are golden.

3. Ladle soup into individual bowls. Sprinkle with French Fried Onions.

Makes 6 servings

Prep Time: 10 minutes
Cook Time: 5 minutes

Italian Tomato and Pasta Soup

5 cups water

2½ cups farfalle (bow tie) or rotini pasta

2 tablespoons dried vegetable flakes, soup greens or dehydrated vegetables

1 tablespoon minced onion

1 teaspoon chicken bouillon granules

1 teaspoon Italian herb seasoning

1 teaspoon sugar

½ teaspoon minced garlic

¼ teaspoon black pepper

1 can (about 28 ounces) crushed tomatoes, undrained

3 cups chopped fresh spinach, rinsed and stemmed

4 to 6 slices crisp-cooked bacon, crumbled

½ cup grated Parmesan cheese

1. Combine water, pasta, vegetable flakes, onion, bouillon, herb seasoning, sugar, garlic and pepper in large saucepan. Bring to a boil over high heat; boil 10 to 12 minutes.

2. Stir in tomatoes with juice, spinach and bacon. Reduce heat; simmer 10 to 12 minutes or until pasta is tender. Sprinkle with cheese. *Makes 4 to 5 servings*

Pizza Meatball and Noodle Soup

1 can (about 14 ounces) beef broth

½ cup chopped onion

½ cup chopped carrot

2 ounces uncooked spaghetti, broken into 2- to 3-inch pieces

1 cup zucchini slices, cut in half

8 ounces frozen fully cooked Italian-style meatballs, thawed

1 can (8 ounces) tomato sauce

½ cup (2 ounces) shredded mozzarella cheese

1. Combine broth, onion, carrot and pasta in large saucepan; bring to a boil. Reduce heat; cover and simmer 3 minutes.

2. Add zucchini, meatballs and tomato sauce to broth mixture; return to a boil. Reduce heat; simmer covered, 8 to 9 minutes or until meatballs are heated through and pasta is tender, stirring frequently. Sprinkle each serving with cheese. *Makes 4 servings*

Hearty Lasagna Soup

1 pound ground beef
¼ cup chopped onion
1 teaspoon minced garlic
¼ teaspoon dried parsley flakes
3½ cups SWANSON® Beef Broth (Regular, 50% Less Sodium or Certified Organic)
1 can (about 14.5 ounces) diced tomatoes
¼ teaspoon dried Italian seasoning, crushed
1½ cups uncooked mafalda or corkscrew-shaped pasta
¼ cup grated Parmesan cheese

1. Cook the beef, onion, garlic and parsley in a 3-quart saucepan over medium-high heat for 10 minutes or until the beef is well browned, stirring often. Pour off any fat.

2. Stir the broth, tomatoes and Italian seasoning into the saucepan and heat to a boil.

3. Stir the pasta in the saucepan. Reduce the heat to medium. Cook for 10 minutes or until the pasta is tender. Stir in the cheese. Serve with additional cheese, if desired.   *Makes 4 servings*

Prep Time: 10 minutes
Cook Time: 25 minutes

Hearty Bean & Pasta Soup

1 cup uncooked elbow macaroni
2 tablespoons olive oil
1 onion, chopped
2 cloves garlic, minced
4 cups water
2 cans (about 14 ounces each) chicken broth
1 jar (about 26 ounces) marinara sauce
1 can (about 15 ounces) Great Northern or cannellini beans, rinsed and drained
1 pound fresh spinach, chopped
2 teaspoons balsamic vinegar

1. Cook macaroni according to package directions. Drain.

2. Meanwhile, heat oil in Dutch oven or large saucepan over medium heat. Add onion and garlic; cook and stir 5 minutes or until onion is tender.

3. Stir in water, broth, marinara sauce and beans; bring to a boil. Reduce heat to low; cook and stir 10 minutes. Stir in spinach, vinegar and pasta; cook 5 minutes.   *Makes 12 servings*

Beef Soup with Noodles

    2 tablespoons soy sauce
    1 teaspoon minced fresh ginger
  ¼ teaspoon red pepper flakes
    1 boneless beef top sirloin steak (about ¾ pound)
    1 tablespoon vegetable or peanut oil
    2 cups sliced fresh mushrooms
    2 cans (about 14 ounces each) beef broth
    1 cup (3 ounces) fresh snow peas, cut diagonally into 1-inch pieces
 1½ cups hot cooked egg noodles (2 ounces uncooked)
    1 green onion, cut diagonally into thin slices
    1 teaspoon dark sesame oil (optional)
       Red bell pepper strips (optional)

1. Combine soy sauce, ginger and pepper flakes in small bowl. Spread mixture evenly over both sides of steak. Marinate 15 minutes.

2. Heat vegetable oil in deep skillet over medium-high heat. Drain steak; reserve marinade (there will only be a small amount of marinade). Add steak to skillet; cook 5 minutes per side.* Let stand on cutting board 10 minutes.

3. Meanwhile, add mushrooms to skillet; stir-fry 2 minutes. Add broth, snow peas and reserved marinade; bring to a boil, scraping up browned bits. Reduce heat to medium-low. Stir in noodles.

4. Cut steak lengthwise in half, then crosswise into thin slices. Stir into soup; heat through. Stir in green onion and sesame oil, if desired. Ladle into soup bowls. Garnish with bell pepper strips. *Makes 4 servings*

*Cooking time is for medium-rare doneness. Adjust time for desired doneness.

Hearty Vegetable Pasta Soup

    1 tablespoon vegetable oil
    1 onion, chopped
    3 cups chicken broth
    1 can (about 14 ounces) diced tomatoes
    1 potato, peeled and cubed
    2 carrots, sliced
    1 stalk celery, sliced
    1 teaspoon dried basil
      Salt and black pepper
  $\frac{1}{3}$ cup uncooked tiny bow tie pasta
    2 ounces fresh spinach, washed, stemmed and chopped

1. Heat oil in Dutch oven over medium-high heat. Cook and stir onion until translucent. Add broth, tomatoes, potato, carrots, celery, basil, salt and pepper; bring to a boil over high heat. Reduce heat to medium-low; simmer uncovered, 20 minutes or until potato and carrots are very tender and flavors are blended, stirring occasionally.

2. Stir in pasta; simmer uncovered, 8 minutes or until pasta is tender.

3. Stir spinach into soup. Simmer uncovered, 2 minutes or until spinach is wilted. Serve immediately. *Makes 6 servings*

Italian Bow Tie Vegetable Soup

    3 cans (14$\frac{1}{2}$ ounces each) chicken broth
    1 can (14$\frac{1}{2}$ ounces) Italian-style or regular stewed tomatoes
  $\frac{1}{2}$ teaspoon Italian seasoning
 1$\frac{1}{2}$ cups (4 ounces) uncooked bow tie pasta (farfalle)
    1 package (about 1 pound) small frozen precooked meatballs
    1 medium zucchini, cut into $\frac{1}{4}$-inch slices
  $\frac{1}{2}$ cup diced red or green bell pepper
 1$\frac{1}{2}$ cups *French's*® French Fried Onions

1. Combine broth, tomatoes and Italian seasoning in large saucepan. Bring to a boil.

2. Stir in pasta, meatballs, zucchini and bell pepper. Simmer for 12 minutes or until pasta is cooked al dente and meatballs are heated through, stirring occasionally. Spoon soup into serving bowls; top with French Fried Onions. *Makes 6 servings*

Prep Time: 5 minutes
Cook Time: 12 minutes

Hearty Vegetable Pasta Soup

Pasta Meatball Soup

10 ounces ground beef

5 tablespoons acini di pepe pasta,* divided

¼ cup fresh bread crumbs

1 egg

2 tablespoons finely chopped fresh parsley, divided

1 teaspoon dried basil, divided

1 clove garlic, minced

¼ teaspoon salt

⅛ teaspoon black pepper

2 cans (about 14 ounces each) beef broth

1 can (about 8 ounces) tomato sauce

⅓ cup chopped onion

*Acini di pepe is tiny rice-shaped pasta. Orzo or pastina can be substituted.

1. Combine beef, 2 tablespoons pasta, bread crumbs, egg, 1 tablespoon parsley, ½ teaspoon basil, garlic, salt and pepper in medium bowl. Shape into 1-inch meatballs.

2. Bring broth, tomato sauce, onion and remaining ½ teaspoon basil to a boil in large saucepan over medium-high heat. Carefully add meatballs to broth. Reduce heat to medium-low; simmer covered, 20 minutes.

3. Add remaining 3 tablespoons pasta; cook 10 minutes or until tender. Garnish with remaining 1 tablespoon parsley.   *Makes 4 servings*

Ginger Wonton Soup

     4 ounces ground pork
     ½ cup ricotta cheese
  1½ teaspoons minced fresh cilantro
     ½ teaspoon black pepper
     ⅛ teaspoon Chinese five-spice powder
   20 wonton wrappers
     1 teaspoon vegetable oil
     ⅓ cup chopped red bell pepper
     1 teaspoon grated fresh ginger
     2 cans (about 14 ounces each) chicken broth
     2 teaspoons soy sauce
     4 ounces fresh pea pods
     1 can (about 9 ounces) baby corn, rinsed and drained
     2 green onions, thinly sliced

1. Cook pork in small nonstick skillet over medium-high heat 4 minutes or until no longer pink. Cool slightly; stir in cheese, cilantro, black pepper and five-spice powder.

2. Place 1 teaspoon filling in center of each wonton wrapper. Fold top corner of wonton over filling. Lightly brush remaining corners with water. Fold left and right corners over filling. Tightly roll filled end toward remaining corner in jelly-roll fashion. Moisten edges with water to seal. Cover and set aside.

3. Heat oil in large saucepan. Add bell pepper and ginger; cook 1 minute. Add broth and soy sauce; bring to a boil. Add pea pods, corn and wontons. Reduce heat to medium-low and simmer 4 to 5 minutes or until wontons are tender. Sprinkle with green onions.

Makes 4 servings

italian classics

Traditional Spaghetti Sauce

12 ounces spaghetti

1 pound mild Italian sausage

½ cup chopped onion

1 can (14.5 ounces) **CONTADINA® Recipe Ready Diced Tomatoes with Roasted Garlic, undrained**

1 cup chicken broth or water

1 can (6 ounces) **CONTADINA Italian Paste with Italian Seasonings**

1 tablespoon chopped fresh parsley

1. Cook pasta according to package directions; drain and keep warm.

2. Crumble sausage into large skillet. Cook over medium-high heat, stirring to break up sausage, 4 to 5 minutes or until no longer pink.

3. Add onion; cook 2 to 3 minutes. Drain.

4. Stir in undrained tomatoes, broth, tomato paste and parsley. Bring to a boil. Reduce heat; cook 10 to 15 minutes or until flavors are blended. Serve sauce over pasta.

Makes 4 to 6 servings

Chicken & Broccoli Alfredo

½ **of a 1-pound package linguine**

1 **cup fresh or frozen broccoli flowerets**

2 **tablespoons butter**

1 **pound skinless, boneless chicken breasts, cut into 1½-inch pieces**

1 **can (10¾ ounces) CAMPBELL'S® Condensed Cream of Mushroom Soup (Regular or 98% Fat Free)**

½ **cup milk**

½ **cup grated Parmesan cheese**

¼ **teaspoon ground black pepper**

1. Prepare the linguine according to the package directions in a 3-quart saucepan. Add the broccoli during the last 4 minutes of cooking. Drain the linguine mixture well in a colander.

2. Heat the butter in a 10-inch skillet over medium-high heat. Add the chicken and cook until it's well browned, stirring often.

3. Stir the soup, milk, cheese, black pepper and linguine mixture in the skillet. Cook until the mixture is hot and bubbling, stirring occasionally. Serve with additional Parmesan cheese.

Makes 4 servings

Prep Time: 10 minutes
Cook Time: 20 minutes

Variation: You can substitute spaghetti or fettuccine for the linguine in this recipe.

Serving Suggestion: Serve with a mixed green salad topped with orange sections, walnut pieces and raspberry vinaigrette. For dessert serve almond biscotti.

Pasta & Potatoes with Pesto

3 **red potatoes, cut into chunks**

8 **ounces uncooked linguine**

¾ **cup frozen peas**

1 **package (about 7 ounces) prepared pesto sauce**

¼ **cup plus 2 tablespoons grated Parmesan cheese, divided**

¼ **teaspoon salt**

¼ **teaspoon black pepper**

1. Place potatoes in medium saucepan; cover with water. Bring to a boil over high heat; reduce heat. Cook uncovered, 10 minutes or until potatoes are tender; drain.

continued on page 222

Chicken & Broccoli Alfredo

Pasta & Potatoes with Pesto, continued

2. Meanwhile, cook pasta according to package directions, adding peas during last 3 minutes of cooking; drain. Return pasta mixture to pan; add potatoes, pesto sauce, 1/4 cup cheese, salt and pepper, tossing until blended.

3. Serve immediately with remaining 2 tablespoons cheese.   *Makes 6 servings*

Tortellini Bake Parmesano

1 package (12 ounces) fresh or frozen cheese tortellini or ravioli
1/2 pound lean ground beef
1/2 medium onion, finely chopped
2 cloves garlic, minced
1/2 teaspoon dried oregano, crushed
1 can (26 ounces) DEL MONTE® Garlic & Herb Chunky Spaghetti Sauce
2 small zucchini, sliced
1/3 cup (about 1 1/2 ounces) grated Parmesan cheese

1. Cook pasta according to package directions; rinse and drain.

2. Meanwhile, brown beef with onion, garlic and oregano in large skillet over medium-high heat; drain. Season with salt and pepper, if desired.

3. Add spaghetti sauce and zucchini. Cook 15 minutes or until thickened, stirring occasionally.

4. Arrange half of pasta in oiled 2-quart microwavable dish; top with half each of sauce and cheese. Repeat layers ending with cheese; cover.

5. Microwave on HIGH 8 to 10 minutes or until heated through, rotating dish halfway through cooking time.   *Makes 4 servings*

Prep and Cook Time: 35 minutes

Hint: For convenience, double the recipe and freeze one half for later use. The recipe can also be made ahead, refrigerated and heated just before serving (allow extra time in microwave if dish is chilled).

Tortellini Bake Parmesano

Spicy Italian Sausage & Penne Pasta

8 ounces uncooked penne pasta
1 pound bulk Italian sausage
1 cup chopped sweet onion
2 cloves garlic, minced
2 cans (about 14 ounces each) seasoned diced tomatoes
3 cups broccoli florets
½ cup shredded Asiago or Romano cheese

1. Cook pasta according to package directions. Drain. Return to saucepan; keep warm.

2. Meanwhile, crumble sausage into large skillet. Add onion; cook and stir over medium-high heat until sausage is cooked through. Drain fat. Add garlic; cook 1 minute. Stir in tomatoes and broccoli. Cover; cook 10 minutes or until broccoli is tender.

3. Add sausage mixture to pasta; toss well. Sprinkle with cheese.   *Makes 4 to 6 servings*

Tip: To add fabulous extra flavor to pasta dishes, slice fresh basil leaves into thin shreds. Sprinkle basil over pasta just before serving.

Baked Ziti

REYNOLDS WRAP® Non-Stick Foil
1 pound ground beef, browned and drained
4 cups (32-ounce jar) chunky garden-style pasta sauce
1 tablespoon Italian seasoning, divided
1 package (16 ounces) ziti pasta, cooked and drained
1 package (8 ounces) shredded mozzarella cheese, divided
1 container (16 ounces) ricotta cheese or cottage cheese
1 egg
¼ cup grated Parmesan cheese, divided

Preheat oven to 350°F.

Combine ground beef, pasta sauce and 2 teaspoons Italian seasoning. Stir pasta into meat sauce; spread half of mixture evenly in pan. Top with half of mozzarella cheese.

continued on page 226

Baked Ziti, continued

Combine ricotta cheese, egg, 2 tablespoons Parmesan cheese and remaining Italian seasoning; spread over mozzarella cheese in pan. Spread remaining pasta mixture over ricotta cheese mixture. Sprinkle with remaining mozzarella and Parmesan cheeses.

Cover with Reynolds Wrap Non-Stick Foil with non-stick (dull) side toward food.

Bake 45 minutes. Remove foil cover and continue baking 15 minutes or until cheese is melted and lightly browned. Let stand 15 minutes before serving.   *Makes 8 servings*

Prep Time: 20 minutes
Cook Time: 1 hour

Spinach Ravioli

   1 package (10 ounces) frozen chopped spinach, thawed and squeezed dry
   1 cup ricotta cheese
   ½ cup grated Romano or Parmesan cheese
   1 egg
   1 tablespoon minced fresh basil
   ½ teaspoon salt
   ½ teaspoon black pepper
   ¼ teaspoon ground nutmeg
   36 wonton wrappers (thawed, if frozen)
   1 jar (about 26 ounces) marinara sauce

1. Combine spinach, cheeses, egg, basil, salt, pepper and nutmeg in medium bowl.

2. Place 1 or 2 wonton wrappers on lightly floured surface, keeping remaining wrappers covered. Place 1 heaping teaspoon filling in center of each wrapper. Moisten edges around filling and place another wrapper on top. Press edges gently around filling to remove air bubbles and seal. Repeat with remaining wrappers.

3. Bring large saucepan of salted water to a boil. Add half of ravioli to boiling water; reduce heat to medium-high. Stir gently and cook until ravioli rise to top (about 3 minutes). Remove ravioli with slotted spoon and keep warm. Repeat with remaining ravioli. Heat marinara sauce in medium saucepan over low heat. Serve pasta with marinara sauce.   *Makes 6 servings*

Vegetable Lasagna

8 uncooked lasagna noodles
  Nonstick cooking spray
2 cups sliced fresh mushrooms
1 cup chopped onion
1 cup chopped green bell pepper
2 cloves garlic, minced
1 can (about 14 ounces) diced tomatoes, drained
1 can (about 8 ounces) tomato sauce, divided
1 teaspoon chopped fresh basil *or* ¼ teaspoon dried basil
1 teaspoon chopped fresh oregano *or* ¼ teaspoon dried oregano
⅛ teaspoon ground red pepper
1½ cups cottage cheese or ricotta cheese
¼ cup grated Romano or Parmesan cheese
2 egg whites
3 tablespoons fine dry bread crumbs
½ (10-ounce) package frozen chopped spinach, thawed and well drained*
¾ cup (3 ounces) shredded mozzarella cheese
¼ cup chopped fresh parsley

Reserve remaining half package for another use, if desired.

1. Prepare noodles according to package directions, omitting salt. Drain. Rinse under cold water. Drain.

2. Coat large skillet with cooking spray. Add mushrooms, onion, bell pepper and garlic; cook and stir over medium heat until vegetables are tender. Stir in diced tomatoes, tomato sauce, basil, oregano and red pepper. Bring to a boil over medium-high heat. Reduce heat to medium-low. Simmer uncovered, 10 minutes, stirring occasionally.

3. Preheat oven to 350°F. Combine cottage cheese, Romano, egg whites and bread crumbs in medium bowl. Stir spinach into cottage cheese mixture. Cut noodles in half crosswise. To prevent sticking, spread 2 tablespoons tomato mixture in bottom of ungreased 8-inch square baking dish. Layer 4 noodles over sauce, overlapping slightly. Top with half of cheese mixture. Layer 4 more noodles over top, slightly overlapping noodles. Top with half of tomato mixture. Repeat layers, ending with tomato sauce mixture.

4. Cover and bake 45 minutes or until hot and bubbly. Sprinkle with mozzarella. Bake uncovered, 2 to 3 minutes more or until cheese melts. Sprinkle with parsley. Let stand 10 minutes before serving. Cut into 4 pieces before serving.   *Makes 4 servings*

Chicken Marsala

  4 cups (6 ounces) uncooked broad egg noodles
½ cup Italian-seasoned dry bread crumbs
  1 teaspoon dried basil
  1 egg
  1 teaspoon water
  4 boneless skinless chicken breasts
  3 tablespoons olive oil, divided
¾ cup chopped onion
  8 ounces cremini or button mushrooms, sliced
  3 cloves garlic, minced
  3 tablespoons all-purpose flour
  1 can (about 14 ounces) chicken broth
½ cup dry marsala wine
¾ teaspoon salt
¼ teaspoon black pepper
  Chopped fresh parsley (optional)

1. Preheat oven to 375°F. Spray 11×7-inch baking dish with nonstick cooking spray.

2. Cook noodles according to package directions. Drain; place in prepared dish.

3. Meanwhile, combine bread crumbs and basil in shallow dish. Beat egg and water in another shallow dish. Dip chicken in egg mixture; shake off excess. Dip chicken into crumb mixture; turn and pat to coat.

4. Heat 2 tablespoons oil in large skillet over medium-high heat. Cook chicken 3 minutes per side or until browned. Transfer to plate.

5. Heat remaining 1 tablespoon oil in same skillet over medium heat. Add onion; cook and stir 5 minutes. Add mushrooms and garlic; cook and stir 3 minutes. Sprinkle mushroom mixture with flour; cook and stir 1 minute. Add broth, wine, salt and pepper; bring to a boil over high heat. Cook and stir 5 minutes or until sauce thickens.

6. Reserve ½ cup sauce. Pour remaining sauce over noodles; stir until noodles are well coated. Place chicken on top of noodles. Spoon reserved sauce over chicken.

7. Bake uncovered, about 20 minutes or until chicken is no longer pink in center and sauce is bubbly and heated through. Sprinkle with parsley. *Makes 4 servings*

Serving Suggestion: Serve with crusty Italian or French bread and a tossed lettuce salad.

Baked Gnocchi

1 package (about 17 ounces) gnocchi

⅓ cup olive oil

3 cloves garlic, minced

1 package (10 ounces) frozen spinach, thawed and squeezed dry

1 can (about 14 ounces) diced tomatoes

1 teaspoon Italian seasoning

Salt and black pepper

½ cup grated Parmesan cheese

½ cup (2 ounces) shredded mozzarella cheese

1. Preheat oven to 350°F. Grease 2½-quart casserole.

2. Cook gnocchi according to package directions. Drain and set aside.

3. Meanwhile, heat oil in large skillet or Dutch oven over medium heat. Add garlic; cook and stir 30 seconds. Stir in spinach; cook covered, 2 minutes or until spinach wilts. Add tomatoes and Italian seasoning. Season with salt and pepper; cook and stir about 5 minutes. Add gnocchi; stir gently.

4. Transfer gnocchi mixture to prepared casserole. Sprinkle with cheeses. Bake 20 to 30 minutes or until casserole is bubbly and cheese is melted. *Makes 4 to 6 servings*

Penne with Creamy Vodka Sauce

2 jars (1 pound 10 ounces each) PREGO® Chunky Tomato, Onion & Garlic Italian Sauce

¼ cup vodka

⅓ cup chopped fresh basil leaves

¼ teaspoon crushed red pepper

½ cup heavy cream

1 package (16 ounces) medium tube-shaped pasta (penne), cooked and drained Grated Parmesan cheese

1. Heat the Italian sauce, vodka, basil and pepper in a 3-quart saucepan over medium heat. Heat to a boil. Remove from the heat and stir in the cream.

2. Put the pasta in a large serving bowl. Pour the sauce mixture over the pasta. Toss to coat. Serve with the cheese. *Makes 4 servings*

Prep Time: 5 minutes
Cook Time: 20 minutes

Manicotti

1 container (16 ounces) ricotta cheese

2 cups (8 ounces) shredded mozzarella cheese

½ cup cottage cheese

2 eggs, beaten

2 tablespoons grated Parmesan cheese

½ teaspoon minced garlic

Salt and black pepper

1 package (about 8 ounces) uncooked manicotti shells

1 pound ground beef

1 jar (about 26 ounces) pasta sauce

2 cups water

1. Preheat oven to 375°F.

2. Combine ricotta, mozzarella, cottage cheese, eggs, Parmesan, garlic, salt and pepper in large bowl; mix well. Fill shells with cheese mixture; place in 13×9-inch baking dish.

3. Brown beef 6 to 8 minutes in large skillet over medium-high heat, stirring to break up meat. Drain fat. Stir in pasta sauce and water (mixture will be thin). Pour sauce over filled manicotti shells.

4. Cover with foil. Bake 1 hour or until sauce is thickened and shells are tender.

Makes 6 servings

tip

To quickly and easily fill the manicotti shells, use a large resealable food storage bag. Spoon the cheese mixture into the bag and cut off one corner. Then simply pipe the mixture into the shells and throw away the bag.

Baked Fusilli with Roasted Vegetables

1 eggplant, cut in half
3 red bell peppers, cut in half
1 sweet onion, cut into quarters
2 tablespoons olive oil
1 container (15 ounces) ricotta cheese
   Salt and black pepper
1 package (about 16 ounces) fusilli pasta, cooked and drained
3 cups (12 ounces) shredded mozzarella cheese
½ cup grated Parmesan cheese

1. Preheat oven to 375°F. Line two baking sheets with foil. Place eggplant, peppers and onion, cut side down, on prepared baking sheets. Brush with olive oil; roast 30 minutes or until tender. Let cool; cut vegetables into bite-size pieces.

2. Combine ricotta and vegetables in large bowl; season with salt and pepper. Add pasta; stir just until combined.

3. Spoon half of pasta mixture into 13×9-inch baking dish. Sprinkle with half of mozzarella and Parmesan. Repeat layers. Bake 25 minutes or until bubbly and browned.

Makes 6 to 8 servings

Cheesy Stuffed Meatballs & Spaghetti

1 pound ground beef
½ cup Italian seasoned dry bread crumbs
1 egg
2 ounces mozzarella cheese, cut into 12 (½-inch) cubes
1 jar (1 pound 10 ounces) RAGÚ® Old World Style® Pasta Sauce
8 ounces spaghetti, cooked and drained

1. In medium bowl, combine ground beef, bread crumbs and egg; shape into 12 meatballs. Press 1 cheese cube into each meatball, enclosing completely.

2. In 3-quart saucepan, bring Pasta Sauce to a boil over medium-high heat. Gently stir in uncooked meatballs.

3. Reduce heat to low and simmer covered, stirring occasionally, 20 minutes or until meatballs are done. Serve over hot spaghetti. Sprinkle, if desired, with grated Parmesan cheese.

Makes 4 servings

Prep Time: 20 minutes
Cook Time: 20 minutes

Pesto Lasagna Rolls

2 cups fresh basil leaves

2 cloves garlic

¾ cup (3 ounces) SARGENTO® Artisan Blends™ Shredded Parmesan Cheese, divided

¾ cup olive oil

2 cups (15 ounces) SARGENTO® Whole Milk Ricotta Cheese*

1 cup (4 ounces) SARGENTO® Shredded Reduced Fat Mozzarella Cheese

1 egg, beaten

1 cup diced zucchini

16 lasagna noodles, cooked, drained and cooled

SARGENTO® Part-Skim Ricotta, Light Ricotta, or Fat Free Ricotta can also be used.

Prepare pesto sauce in covered blender or food processor by processing basil with garlic until chopped. Add ½ cup Parmesan cheese; process until well mixed. With machine running, slowly add oil and continue processing until smooth. Set aside. In medium bowl, combine Ricotta and Mozzarella cheeses, remaining ¼ cup Parmesan cheese and egg; blend well. Fold in zucchini. Spread 2 heaping tablespoons cheese mixture on each lasagna noodle. Roll up each noodle individually and stand vertically in greased 11×7-inch baking dish. Pour pesto sauce over lasagna rolls; cover and bake at 350°F 40 minutes or until bubbly and heated through.

Makes 8 servings

Cheesy Chicken & Broccoli Fettuccine

1 to 2 tablespoons olive oil

1 pound boneless skinless chicken breasts, cut into 1-inch pieces

2 boxes (10 ounces each) frozen broccoli with cheese sauce, defrosted

1 package (12 ounces) fresh fettuccine, cooked and drained

Salt and black pepper

1. Heat oil in large skillet over medium-high heat. Add chicken; cook and stir about 10 minutes or until cooked through.

2. Stir in broccoli and cheese sauce; heat until crisp-tender.

3. Add pasta; stir to coat with cheese mixture. Season with salt and pepper.

Makes 8 servings

Extras: Try using your favorite flavor of fresh fettuccine to add additional zest to your dish. Fresh pasta cooks in a fraction of the time that boxed pasta cooks.

Baked Ravioli with Pumpkin Sauce

1 package (9 ounces) refrigerated cheese ravioli
1 tablespoon butter
1 shallot, finely chopped
1 cup whipping cream
1 cup solid-pack pumpkin
½ cup shredded Asiago cheese, divided
½ teaspoon salt
¼ teaspoon ground nutmeg
⅛ teaspoon black pepper
½ cup coarse plain dry bread crumbs or small croutons

1. Preheat oven to 350°F. Grease 2-quart baking dish. Cook pasta according to package directions. Drain well; cover and keep warm.

2. Meanwhile, melt butter in medium saucepan over medium heat. Add shallot; cook and stir 3 minutes or until tender. Reduce heat to low. Add cream, pumpkin, ¼ cup Asiago, salt, nutmeg and pepper; cook and stir 2 minutes or until cheese melts. Gently stir in pasta.

3. Transfer pasta and sauce to prepared baking dish. Combine remaining ¼ cup Asiago and bread crumbs in small bowl; sprinkle over ravioli.

4. Bake 15 minutes or until heated through and topping is lightly browned.   *Makes 4 servings*

Contadina® Classic Lasagne

1 pound dry lasagne noodles, cooked
1 tablespoon olive or vegetable oil
1 cup chopped onion
½ cup chopped green bell pepper
2 cloves garlic, minced
1½ pounds lean ground beef
2 cans (14.5 ounces each) CONTADINA® Recipe Ready Diced Tomatoes, undrained
1 can (8 ounces) CONTADINA Tomato Sauce
1 can (6 ounces) CONTADINA Tomato Paste
½ cup dry red wine or beef broth
1½ teaspoons salt
1 teaspoon dried oregano leaves, crushed
1 teaspoon dried basil leaves, crushed
½ teaspoon ground black pepper
1 egg
1 cup (8 ounces) ricotta cheese
2 cups (8 ounces) shredded mozzarella cheese, divided

1. Cook pasta according to package directions; drain.

2. Meanwhile, heat oil in large skillet. Add onion, bell pepper and garlic; sauté for 3 minutes or until vegetables are tender.

3. Add beef; cook for 5 to 6 minutes or until evenly browned.

4. Add undrained tomatoes, tomato sauce, tomato paste, wine, salt, oregano, basil and black pepper; bring to a boil. Reduce heat to low; simmer, uncovered, for 20 minutes, stirring occasionally.

5. Beat egg slightly in medium bowl. Stir in ricotta cheese and 1 cup mozzarella cheese.

6. Layer one third of noodles, half of meat sauce, one third of noodles, all of ricotta cheese mixture, remaining noodles and remaining meat sauce in ungreased 13×9-inch baking dish. Sprinkle with remaining mozzarella cheese.

7. Bake in preheated 350°F oven for 25 to 30 minutes or until heated through. Let stand for 10 minutes before cutting. *Makes 10 servings*

Prep Time: 35 minutes
Cook Time: 30 minutes
Stand Time: 10 minutes

go for the grain

Asiago and Asparagus Risotto-Style Rice

    2 **cups chopped onion**
    1 **can (about 14 ounces) chicken broth**
    1 **cup uncooked converted rice**
    2 **garlic cloves, minced**
$\frac{1}{2}$ **pound asparagus spears, trimmed and broken into 1-inch pieces**
    1 **to 1$\frac{1}{4}$ cups half-and-half, divided**
$\frac{1}{2}$ **cup (about 4 ounces) shredded Asiago cheese, plus additional for garnish**
$\frac{1}{4}$ **cup ($\frac{1}{2}$ stick) butter, cut into small pieces**
    2 **ounces pine nuts or slivered almonds, toasted**
    1 **teaspoon salt**

Slow Cooker Directions

1. Combine onion, broth, rice and garlic in 3$\frac{1}{2}$- to 4-quart slow cooker. Stir until well blended; cover and cook 2 hours on HIGH or until rice is tender.

2. Stir in asparagus and $\frac{1}{2}$ cup half-and-half. Cover and cook 20 to 30 minutes more or until asparagus is crisp-tender.

3. Stir in $\frac{1}{2}$ cup cheese, butter, nuts and salt; cover and let stand 5 minutes to allow cheese to melt slightly. Fluff with fork and garnish with additional cheese before serving.

Makes 4 servings

Prep Time: 20 minutes
Cook Time: 2$\frac{1}{2}$ hours

Barley Vegetable Casserole

$2\frac{1}{4}$ **cups vegetable broth, divided**
$\frac{2}{3}$ **cup uncooked barley (not quick-cooking)**
4 cups frozen mixed vegetables (broccoli, cauliflower, carrots and onions)
$\frac{1}{2}$ **teaspoon garlic powder**
$\frac{1}{4}$ **teaspoon black pepper**
$\frac{1}{2}$ **teaspoon butter**
$\frac{1}{2}$ **teaspoon salt**

1. Preheat oven to 350°F. Spray 1-quart casserole with nonstick cooking spray.

2. Place $\frac{1}{4}$ cup broth and barley in nonstick skillet; cook over medium heat 3 minutes or until lightly browned, stirring frequently. Transfer to prepared casserole.

3. Add vegetables, garlic powder, pepper and remaining 2 cups broth to casserole; mix well.

4. Cover and bake 50 minutes or until barley is tender and most liquid is absorbed, stirring several times during baking. Stir in butter and salt. Let stand 5 minutes before serving.

Makes 4 servings

South-of-the-Border Rice and Beans

$1\frac{1}{4}$ **cups water**
1 cup ORTEGA® Salsa, any variety
$\frac{1}{2}$ **packet (3 tablespoons) ORTEGA® Taco Seasoning Mix**
2 teaspoons vegetable oil
2 cups uncooked instant white rice
1 can (about 15 ounces) pinto beans, rinsed, drained
$\frac{1}{4}$ **cup chopped cilantro**

COMBINE water, salsa, seasoning mix and oil in large saucepan; mix well. Stir in rice and beans; mix well.

BRING to a boil over medium-high heat. Cover; remove from heat. Let stand 5 minutes.

STIR in cilantro.

Makes 4 servings

Barley Vegetable Casserole

Polenta-Style Corn Casserole

1 can (about 14 ounces) vegetable or chicken broth
½ cup cornmeal
1 can (about 7 ounces) corn, drained
1 can (about 4 ounces) diced green chiles, drained
¼ cup diced red bell pepper
½ teaspoon salt
¼ teaspoon black pepper
1 cup (4 ounces) shredded Cheddar cheese

Slow Cooker Directions

1. Pour broth into slow cooker. Whisk in cornmeal. Add corn, chiles, bell pepper, salt and black pepper; cover and cook on LOW 4 to 5 hours or on HIGH 2 to 3 hours.

2. Stir in cheese. Cook uncovered, 15 to 30 minutes or until cheese melts.   *Makes 6 servings*

Serving Suggestion: Divide cooked corn mixture into lightly greased individual ramekins or spread in pie plate; cover and refrigerate. Serve at room temperature or warm in oven or microwave.

Fried Rice

1 tablespoon vegetable oil
3 eggs, lightly beaten
1 can (14½ ounces) chicken broth
1 package (16 ounces) frozen stir-fry vegetables, thawed
2 tablespoons soy sauce
2 cups MINUTE® White Rice, uncooked

Heat oil in large nonstick skillet over medium heat. Add eggs; scramble until done. Remove from skillet; cover to keep warm.

Add broth, vegetables and soy sauce to skillet; bring to a boil. Stir in rice; cover. Remove from heat. Let stand 5 minutes.

Stir in scrambled eggs. Serve immediately.   *Makes 4 servings*

Couscous Primavera

Nonstick cooking spray
1 shallot, minced or ¼ cup minced red onion
8 spears fresh asparagus, cooked and cut into 1-inch pieces
1 cup frozen peas
1 cup halved grape tomatoes
½ cup water
⅛ teaspoon salt
⅛ teaspoon black pepper
6 tablespoons uncooked whole wheat couscous
¼ cup grated Parmesan cheese

1. Coat large skillet with cooking spray. Add shallot; cook over medium-high heat 3 minutes or until tender. Add asparagus and peas; cook 2 minutes or until peas are heated through. Add tomatoes; cook 2 minutes or until softened. Add water, salt and pepper; bring to a boil.

2. Stir in couscous. Reduce heat to low; cover and simmer 2 minutes or until liquid is absorbed. Fluff with fork. Stir in cheese. Serve immediately. *Makes 2 servings*

Vegetable Medley Rice Pilaf

Nonstick cooking spray
1 red onion or 1 shallot, chopped
1 carrot, shredded
1 cup fresh broccoli florets
1 cup instant brown rice
1 teaspoon olive oil
¼ teaspoon dried thyme
1 cup vegetable or chicken broth
⅛ teaspoon black pepper

1. Spray large skillet with cooking spray. Add onion, carrot and broccoli; cook and stir over medium heat 5 to 8 minutes or until crisp-tender. Add rice, oil, and thyme; cook and stir 1 minute to coat rice with oil.

2. Stir in broth; bring to a boil. Reduce heat to low; cover and simmer 5 minutes. Remove from heat; set aside 5 minutes. Fluff with fork and season with pepper before serving.

Makes 4 servings

Toasted Corn & Sage Harvest Risotto

1 tablespoon olive oil

1 cup fresh or drained canned whole kernel corn

1 large orange or red pepper, chopped (about 1 cup)

1 medium onion, chopped (about ½ cup)

1¾ cups uncooked regular long-grain white rice

4 cups SWANSON® Chicken Broth (Regular, Natural Goodness® or Certified Organic)

1 teaspoon ground sage

1 can (10¾ ounces) CAMPBELL'S® Condensed Cream of Celery Soup (Regular or 98% Fat Free)

¼ cup grated Parmesan cheese

1. Heat the oil in a 4-quart saucepan over medium heat. Add the corn, pepper and onion and cook for 5 minutes or until the vegetables are lightly browned.

2. Add the rice to the saucepan and cook and stir for 30 seconds. Stir in the broth and sage and heat to a boil. Reduce the heat to low. Cover and cook for 20 minutes or until the rice is tender.

3. Stir in the soup. Cook for 2 minutes or until the rice mixture is hot. Sprinkle with the cheese.

Makes 6 servings

Prep Time: 15 minutes
Cook Time: 35 minutes

tip

If you would like a delicious meatless side dish, substitute SWANSON® Vegetable Broth (Regular or Certified Organic) for the Chicken Broth.

Toasted Corn & Sage Harvest Risotto

Sweet Potato, Wild and White Rice Dressing

½ cup (1 stick) butter

2 cups chopped onions

1½ cups chopped celery

3 cloves garlic, finely chopped

½ teaspoon ground ginger

½ teaspoon ground sage

¼ teaspoon dried rosemary

¼ teaspoon ground cinnamon

2 sweet potatoes (12 ounces each), cooked and cut into ½-inch cubes

1 package (14 ounces) country-style stuffing mix

1½ cups cooked white rice

1 cup golden raisins

1 cup toasted pecans, coarsely chopped

1 cup cooked wild rice

¾ teaspoon salt

½ teaspoon black pepper

1 can (about 14 ounces) chicken broth

1. Preheat oven to 350°F. Grease 13×9-inch baking dish.

2. Melt butter in large nonstick skillet over medium-high heat. Add onions, celery, garlic, ginger, sage, rosemary and cinnamon; cook and stir 6 to 8 minutes or until onions are tender. Transfer to large bowl.

3. Add sweet potatoes, stuffing mix, white rice, raisins, pecans, wild rice, salt and pepper to onion mixture. Toss gently to blend. Drizzle broth over stuffing mixture; toss gently to moisten. Transfer to prepared dish.

4. Bake covered, 30 minutes or until heated through. Uncover; bake 30 minutes or until top is browned.

Makes 8 servings

Buckwheat with Zucchini and Mushrooms

1½ to 2 tablespoons olive oil
1 cup sliced mushrooms
1 zucchini, cut into ½-inch pieces
1 onion, chopped
1 clove garlic, minced
¾ cup buckwheat
¼ teaspoon dried thyme
¼ teaspoon salt
⅛ teaspoon black pepper
1¼ cups vegetable or chicken broth
Lemon wedges (optional)

1. Heat oil in large nonstick skillet over medium heat. Add mushrooms, zucchini, onion and garlic; cook and stir 7 to 10 minutes or until vegetables are tender. Add buckwheat, thyme, salt and pepper; cook and stir 2 minutes.

2. Add broth; bring to a boil. Cover; reduce heat to low. Cook 10 to 13 minutes or until liquid is absorbed and buckwheat is tender. Remove from heat; let stand covered, 5 minutes. Serve with lemon wedges, if desired.
Makes 4 to 6 servings

tip

For a different flavor, add pancetta to this dish. Coarsely chop 4 slices pancetta and cook in medium skillet over medium heat about 5 minutes to render fat. Add 1 tablespoon olive oil, mushrooms, zucchini, onion and garlic. Proceed as directed above.

Country Polenta

4 cups water
½ teaspoon salt (optional)
2 cups CREAM OF WHEAT® Hot Cereal (Instant, 1-minute, 2½-minute or 10-minute cook time), uncooked, divided
⅓ cup grated Parmesan cheese
¼ teaspoon crushed red pepper
¼ teaspoon dried basil
¼ teaspoon ground black pepper
3 tablespoons vegetable oil

1. Coat 8-inch square pan generously with nonstick cooking spray. Bring water and salt, if desired, to a boil. Gradually add 1 cup Cream of Wheat, stirring constantly with wire whisk until well blended. Return to a boil. Reduce heat to low; simmer, uncovered, as directed on package or until thickened, stirring frequently. Cool slightly.

2. Add cheese, red pepper, basil and black pepper; mix well. Pour Cream of Wheat mixture evenly into prepared pan; cover. Refrigerate at least 2 hours or until set.

3. Toast remaining 1 cup Cream of Wheat in large skillet over medium-low heat until golden brown, stirring frequently. Remove from heat. Cut chilled polenta into 12 triangles. Coat both sides generously with toasted Cream of Wheat.

4. Heat oil in large skillet over medium heat. Cook polenta triangles 3 to 4 minutes on each side or until crisp and golden brown. Serve immediately. *Makes 6 servings*

Prep Time: 15 minutes
Start to Finish Time: 2 hours, 25 minutes

Variation: Prepared Cream of Wheat mixture can be poured into pan, tightly covered and refrigerated up to 24 hours before being cut into triangles. Coat with toasted cereal; proceed as directed.

Whole Wheat Kugel

1¼ teaspoons salt, divided
8 ounces whole wheat linguine
1 container (15 ounces) ricotta cheese
1 cup sour cream
¼ cup sugar
¼ teaspoon ground cinnamon, plus additional for garnish
3 eggs

1. Preheat oven to 350°F. Grease 8-inch square glass baking dish; set aside.

2. Fill large saucepan with water. Add 1 teaspoon salt; bring to a boil over high heat. Break pasta into pieces about 3 inches long; stir into boiling water. Cook over high heat until tender, about 10 minutes. Drain well.

3. Meanwhile, combine ricotta, sour cream, sugar, ¼ teaspoon cinnamon and remaining ¼ teaspoon salt in large bowl. Add eggs; beat until smooth. Add pasta; mix well. Spoon into prepared dish.

4. Bake 45 to 50 minutes or until firm and lightly browned on top. Sprinkle with additional cinnamon.

Makes 9 servings

Quinoa and Roasted Corn

   1 cup uncooked quinoa

   2 cups water

   ½ teaspoon salt

   4 ears corn *or* 2 cups frozen corn

   ¼ cup plus 1 tablespoon vegetable oil, divided

   1 cup chopped green onions, divided

   1 teaspoon coarse salt

   1 cup quartered grape tomatoes or chopped plum tomatoes, drained*

   1 cup black beans, rinsed and drained

   ¼ teaspoon grated lime peel

      Juice of 1 lime (about 2 tablespoons)

   ¼ teaspoon sugar

   ¼ teaspoon cumin

   ¼ teaspoon black pepper

Place tomatoes in fine-mesh strainer and place over bowl 10 to 15 minutes.

1. Place quinoa in fine-mesh strainer; rinse well under cold running water. Transfer to medium saucepan; add water and salt. Bring to a boil over high heat. Reduce heat; cover and simmer 15 to 18 minutes or until water is absorbed and quinoa is tender. Transfer quinoa to large bowl.

2. Meanwhile, remove husks and silk from corn; cut kernels off cobs. Heat ¼ cup oil in large skillet over medium-high heat. Add corn; cook 10 to 12 minutes or until tender and light brown, stirring occasionally. Stir in ⅔ cup green onions and coarse salt; cook and stir 2 minutes. Add corn to quinoa. Gently stir in tomatoes and black beans.

3. Combine lime peel, lime juice, sugar, cumin and black pepper in small bowl. Whisk in remaining 1 tablespoon oil until blended. Pour over quinoa mixture; toss lightly to coat. Sprinkle with remaining ⅓ cup green onions. Serve warm or chilled.   *Makes 6 to 8 servings*

Creamy Souper Rice

**1 can (10¾ ounces) CAMPBELL'S® Condensed Cream of Mushroom Soup
(Regular or 98% Fat Free)**
1½ cups SWANSON® Natural Goodness® Chicken Broth
1½ cups uncooked instant white rice
1 tablespoon grated Parmesan cheese
Freshly ground black pepper

1. Heat the soup and broth in a 2-quart saucepan over medium heat to a boil.

2. Stir the rice and cheese in the saucepan. Cover the saucepan and remove from the heat. Let stand for 5 minutes. Fluff the rice with a fork. Serve with the black pepper and additional Parmesan cheese.   *Makes 4 servings*

Prep Time: 5 minutes
Cook Time: 10 minutes
Stand Time: 5 minutes

Kitchen Tip: Any of CAMPBELL'S® Condensed Cream Soups will work in this recipe: Cream of Chicken, Cream of Celery, even Cheddar Cheese.

Bulgur Pilaf with Tomato and Zucchini

1 cup uncooked bulgur wheat
1 tablespoon olive oil
¾ cup chopped onion
2 cloves garlic, minced
1 can (about 14 ounces) whole tomatoes, drained and coarsely chopped
½ pound zucchini, thinly sliced
1 cup chicken broth
1 teaspoon dried basil
⅛ teaspoon black pepper

1. Rinse bulgur thoroughly under cold water, removing any debris. Drain well; set aside.

2. Heat oil in large saucepan over medium heat. Add onion and garlic; cook and stir 3 minutes or until onion is tender. Stir in tomatoes and zucchini; reduce heat to medium-low. Cook covered, 15 minutes or until zucchini is almost tender, stirring occasionally.

3. Stir bulgur, broth, basil and pepper into vegetable mixture. Bring to a boil over high heat. Reduce heat to low. Cook covered, over low heat 15 minutes or until bulgur is tender and liquid is almost completely absorbed, stirring occasionally. Remove from heat; let stand covered, 10 minutes. Stir gently before serving.   *Makes 8 servings*

sensational salads

Garden Fresh Salad

5 cups assorted lettuce
½ cup bell pepper slices
½ cup cherry or grape tomatoes
½ cucumber, sliced
½ red onion, sliced
¼ cup sliced radishes
  Fresh thyme or parsley
  Bottled dressing

1. Divide lettuce, pepper, tomatoes, cucumber, onion, radishes and thyme evenly among bowls. Top with dressing.   *Makes 4 servings*

Sweet & Tangy Coleslaw

1 small bag (16 ounces) shredded cabbage
½ cup mayonnaise
½ cup *French's*® Honey Mustard

1. Combine ingredients in large bowl until blended.

2. Chill until ready to serve.   *Makes 6 to 8 servings*

Prep Time: 5 minutes

Mixed Greens with Pecans, Cranberries & Goat Cheese

⅓ cup extra-virgin olive oil

2 tablespoons balsamic or cider vinegar

1 tablespoon sugar

¼ teaspoon salt

⅛ teaspoon red pepper flakes

1 package (5 ounces) mixed greens

½ cup pecans, toasted

⅓ cup thinly sliced red onion

⅓ cup dried cranberries

2 ounces crumbled goat cheese

1. Combine oil, vinegar, sugar, salt and pepper flakes in small bowl. Whisk until well blended.

2. Combine greens, pecans, onion, cranberries and dressing in serving bowl; toss gently. Sprinkle with cheese.

Makes 6 to 8 servings

Roasted Vegetable Salad

¼ pound DOLE® Asparagus, trimmed

1 portobello mushroom, cut into slices (about ¼ pound)

1 red or green bell pepper, cut into slices

½ cup cherry or grape tomatoes

½ small red onion, cut into slices

2 tablespoons olive oil

Salt and freshly ground pepper, to taste

1 package (5 ounces) DOLE® Baby Romaine Blend or other DOLE Salad variety

¼ cup balsamic vinaigrette dressing

⅓ cup shaved Parmesan cheese

• Place cut vegetables on baking sheet lined with foil.

• Sprinkle oil, salt and pepper over vegetables; toss to coat evenly.

• Bake at 450°F., 10 to 15 minutes or until vegetables are tender.

• Toss salad blend with dressing to coat. Arrange roasted vegetables decoratively on top of Romaine. Garnish with shaved Parmesan.

Makes 3 to 4 servings

Prep Time: 20 minutes

Mixed Greens with Pecans, Cranberries & Goat Cheese

Lime-Ginger Cole Slaw

        2 cups shredded green cabbage
    1½ cups matchstick-size carrots
        1 cup shredded red cabbage
        ¼ cup finely chopped green onions
        3 tablespoons lime juice
        2 tablespoons sugar
        2 tablespoons chopped fresh cilantro
        2 teaspoons vegetable or canola oil
    1½ teaspoons grated fresh ginger
        ⅛ teaspoon salt
        ⅛ teaspoon red pepper flakes

1. Combine all ingredients in large bowl; toss well.
2. Let stand 10 minutes before serving.

Makes 4 servings

Roasted Pepper and Avocado Salad

        2 red bell peppers
        2 orange bell peppers
        2 yellow bell peppers
        2 ripe avocados, halved, pitted and peeled
        3 shallots, thinly sliced
        ¼ cup FILIPPO BERIO® Extra Virgin Olive Oil
        1 clove garlic, crushed
            Finely grated peel and juice of 1 lemon
            Salt and freshly ground black pepper

Place bell peppers on baking sheet. Broil, 4 to 5 inches from heat, 5 minutes on each side or until entire surface of each bell pepper is blistered and blackened slightly. Place bell peppers in paper bag. Close bag; cool 15 to 20 minutes. Cut around cores of bell peppers; twist and remove. Cut bell peppers lengthwise in half. Peel off skin with paring knife; rinse under cold water to remove seeds. Slice bell peppers into ½-inch-thick strips; place in shallow dish. Cut avocados into ¼-inch-thick slices; add to bell peppers. Sprinkle with shallots.

In small bowl, whisk together olive oil, garlic, lemon peel and juice. Pour over bell pepper mixture. Cover; refrigerate at least 1 hour before serving. Season to taste with salt and black pepper.

Makes 6 servings

Mixed Greens and Fruit Salad with Warm Onion Vinaigrette

3 tablespoons olive oil

¼ cup finely chopped shallots or sweet onion

1 cup SWANSON® Chicken Broth (Regular, Natural Goodness® or Certified Organic)

2 tablespoons balsamic vinegar

¼ cup packed brown sugar

1 tablespoon coarse-grain Dijon-style mustard

2 bags (5 to 8 ounces each) mixed salad greens

2 ripe pears or apples, thinly sliced (about 2 cups)

½ cup dried cherries or cranberries

¼ cup pecans, toasted

Crumbled blue cheese (optional)

1. Heat **1 tablespoon** oil in a 2-quart saucepan over medium heat. Add the shallots and cook for 3 minutes or until they're tender.

2. Stir the broth, vinegar, brown sugar and mustard in the saucepan and heat to a boil. Cook for 5 minutes or until the mixture is slightly reduced. Remove the saucepan from the heat. Beat the remaining oil into the broth mixture with a fork or whisk. Remove the saucepan from the heat and cool slightly.

3. Toss the salad greens with ½ **cup** dressing in a large bowl. Arrange the greens on a serving platter. Top with the pears, cherries, pecans and cheese, if desired. Serve with the remaining dressing.   *Makes 8 servings*

Prep Time: 10 minutes
Cook Time: 15 minutes

Grilled Tri-Colored Pepper Salad

1 *each* red, yellow and green bell pepper, cut into halves or quarters
1/3 cup extra-virgin olive oil
3 tablespoons balsamic vinegar
2 cloves garlic, minced
1/4 teaspoon salt
1/4 teaspoon black pepper
1/3 cup crumbled goat cheese (about 1 1/2 ounces)
1/4 cup thinly sliced fresh basil leaves

1. Prepare grill for direct cooking.

2. Place bell peppers, skin side down, on grid over high heat. Grill covered, 10 to 12 minutes or until skin is charred. Place charred bell peppers in paper bag. Close bag; set aside to cool 10 to 15 minutes. Remove skin; discard.

3. Place bell peppers in shallow glass serving dish. Combine oil, vinegar, garlic, salt and black pepper in small bowl; whisk until well blended. Pour over bell peppers. Let stand 30 minutes at room temperature. (Or cover and refrigerate up to 24 hours. Bring bell peppers to room temperature before serving.)

4. Sprinkle bell peppers with cheese and basil just before serving. *Makes 4 to 6 servings*

Mediterranean Chop Salad

3 ribs celery, sliced *or* 1 cup sliced fennel
1 cup chopped roasted red or yellow peppers
1 large seedless cucumber, peeled and chopped
1/2 cup chopped pitted ripe olives
1/2 cup prepared balsamic vinaigrette salad dressing
1 package (12 ounces) hearts of romaine, rinsed and chopped
1 box (6 ounces) PEPPERIDGE FARM® Seasoned Croutons or any variety
Freshly ground black pepper
Parmesan cheese shavings

1. Stir the celery, peppers, cucumber, olives and dressing in a large serving bowl. Cover and refrigerate until serving time.

2. Toss the chopped lettuce, croutons and dressing mixture just before serving. Sprinkle with the black pepper and Parmesan cheese. *Makes 8 servings*

Prep Time: 25 minutes

Grilled Tri-Colored Pepper Salad

Cool Summer Gazpacho Salad

3 cups fresh DOLE® Tropical Gold® Pineapple, cut into chunks
2 cups chopped tomatoes, drained
1 large cucumber, halved lengthwise and thinly sliced
¼ cup chopped green onions
¼ cup red wine vinegar
4 teaspoons olive or vegetable oil
½ teaspoon dried basil leaves, crushed

Stir together pineapple and remaining ingredients in large bowl. Cover; chill 1 hour or overnight to blend flavors. Stir before serving. *Makes 10 servings*

Prep Time: 20 minutes
Chill Time: 1 hour

Best 'Cue Cole Slaw

⅓ cup dill pickle relish
⅓ cup vegetable oil
3 tablespoons lime juice
2 tablespoons honey
1 teaspoon salt
1 teaspoon ground cumin
1 teaspoon ground red pepper
1 teaspoon black pepper
1 head green cabbage, very thinly sliced
2 carrots, shredded
1 bunch green onions, sliced
5 radishes, sliced

1. Combine relish, oil, lime juice, honey, salt, cumin, red pepper and black pepper in large bowl. Add cabbage, carrots, green onions and radishes; stir until well combined.

2. Chill at least 1 hour before serving. *Makes 6 to 8 servings*

Variation: For a sweeter taste, add slivered apples instead of the dill pickle relish.

Bell Pepper Salad

3 tablespoons olive oil
2 *each* red, green and yellow bell peppers, cut into strips
2 cups thinly sliced red onion
1 cup salsa
3 cups torn lettuce
½ teaspoon salt
¼ teaspoon black pepper

1. Heat oil in large skillet over medium heat. Cook and stir bell peppers and onion about 10 minutes or until tender. Add salsa; cook and stir until heated through. Cool slightly.

2. Place mixture in large bowl; cover with plastic wrap. Refrigerate at least 2 hours or overnight to allow flavors to blend.

3. Serve pepper mixture over lettuce. Season with salt and black pepper. *Makes 8 servings*

Mixed Greens with Raspberry Vinaigrette

½ cup walnuts
⅓ cup vegetable oil
2½ tablespoons raspberry vinegar
1 tablespoon chopped shallot
½ teaspoon salt
½ teaspoon sugar
2 cups washed and torn Romaine lettuce
2 cups washed and torn spinach
2 cups washed and torn red leaf lettuce
1 cup halved red seedless grapes

1. Preheat oven to 350°F. Spread walnuts in single layer on baking sheet. Bake 6 to 8 minutes or until light golden brown, stirring frequently; cool. Coarsely chop; set aside.

2. Place oil, vinegar, shallot, salt and sugar in small bowl; whisk until well blended. Cover; refrigerate up to 1 week.

3. Combine Romaine, spinach, red leaf lettuce, grapes and walnuts in large bowl. Just before serving, add dressing; toss well to coat. *Makes 6 to 8 servings*

Goat Cheese, Citrus & Tomato Salad

1 large orange, peeled
1 large grapefruit, peeled
1 large tomato, cut into thin wedges
4 large fresh basil leaves, thinly sliced (optional)
½ cup WISH-BONE® Italian Dressing
1 package (4 ounces) watercress, stems removed, or mixed salad greens
1 container (4 ounces) goat cheese crumbles
⅛ teaspoon ground black pepper
¼ cup chopped candied pecans or walnuts

Section orange and grapefruit over medium bowl, reserving any juices. Add segments to reserved juices. Stir in tomato, basil and WISH-BONE® Italian Dressing.

Arrange watercress on serving platter, then top with citrus mixture. Sprinkle with cheese, black pepper and pecans. *Makes 4 servings*

Prep Time: 15 minutes

tip

Create your own signature salad dressing. Add a touch of Dijon or honey mustard to your WISH-BONE® Italian Dressing and enjoy!

Nine-Layer Salad

6 cups baby spinach, packed
1½ cups grape tomatoes
2 cups pattypan squash, halved crosswise
1 cup peas, blanched
4 ounces baby corn, halved lengthwise
2 cups baby carrots, blanched and halved lengthwise
1 cup peppercorn-ranch salad dressing
1 cup shredded Cheddar cheese
4 strips bacon

1. Layer spinach, tomatoes, squash, peas, corn and carrots in 4-quart glass bowl. Pour dressing over salad; spread evenly. Top with cheese. Cover and refrigerate 4 hours.

2. Cook bacon in medium skillet over medium-high heat until crispy. Crumble and sprinkle over top of salad. *Makes 7 servings*

Classic Coleslaw

1 cup HELLMANN'S® or BEST FOODS® Real Mayonnaise*
3 tablespoons lemon juice
2 tablespoons sugar
1 teaspoon salt
6 cups shredded cabbage
1 cup shredded carrots
½ cup chopped green bell pepper

*Also terrific with HELLMANN'S® or BEST FOODS® Light or Canola Cholesterol Free Mayonnaise.

Combine HELLMANN'S® or BEST FOODS® Real Mayonnaise, lemon juice, sugar and salt in large bowl. Stir in cabbage, carrots and bell pepper. Chill, if desired. *Makes 12 servings*

Prep Time: 10 minutes

Spinach Salad with Beets

6 cups (6 ounces) packed baby spinach or torn spinach leaves
1 cup canned pickled julienned beets, drained
¼ cup thinly sliced red onion, separated into rings
¼ cup croutons
⅓ cup raspberry vinaigrette salad dressing
¼ cup crumbled cooked bacon
Black pepper (optional)

1. Combine spinach, beets, onion and croutons. Add dressing; toss to coat.

2. Divide evenly among plates. Sprinkle with bacon and pepper, if desired.   *Makes 4 servings*

tip

Nothing tops a salad better than fresh, crunchy croutons! Place about 2 cups of fresh bread cubes into a microwavable dish. Heat on HIGH 2½ to 3 minutes or until bread cubes are dry, stirring two or three times during heating. Let stand 2 minutes. Season with herbs and/or cheese as desired.

Harvest Salad

2 packages (about 7 ounces each) mixed salad greens (about 8 cups)
2 cups cut-up fresh vegetables (red onion, cucumber and carrot)
1 can (10¾ ounces) CAMPBELL'S® Condensed Tomato Soup (Regular, Healthy Request®)
¼ cup vegetable oil
¼ cup red wine vinegar
1 tablespoon honey or sugar
1 package (0.7 ounces) Italian salad dressing mix
1 box (5.5 ounces) PEPPERIDGE FARM® Croutons, any variety
¼ cup shelled pumpkin or sunflower seeds

1. Mix the salad greens and vegetables in a large bowl.

2. Beat the soup, oil, vinegar, honey and salad dressing mix with a fork or whisk in a small bowl. Pour **¾ cup** of the soup mixture over the salad mixture and toss to coat.

3. Arrange the salad on a serving platter. Top with the croutons and pumpkin seeds. Serve immediately with the remaining soup mixture. *Makes 8 servings*

Prep Time: 10 minutes

Jalapeño Cole Slaw

6 cups shredded cabbage or coleslaw mix
2 tomatoes, seeded and chopped
6 green onions, coarsely chopped
2 jalapeño peppers, finely chopped*
¼ cup cider vinegar
3 tablespoons honey
1 teaspoon salt

*Jalapeño peppers can sting and irritate the skin, so wear rubber gloves when handling peppers and do not touch your eyes. For a milder cole slaw, discard seeds and veins when chopping the jalapeños.

1. Combine cabbage, tomatoes, green onions, jalapeños, vinegar, honey and salt in large serving bowl; mix well. Cover; refrigerate at least 2 hours.

2. Stir well before serving. *Makes 4 servings*

vegetable bounty

Asparagus with No-Cook Creamy Mustard Sauce

Creamy Mustard Sauce
$\frac{1}{2}$ **cup plain yogurt**
2 **tablespoons mayonnaise**
1 **tablespoon Dijon mustard**
2 **teaspoons lemon juice**
$\frac{1}{2}$ **teaspoon salt**

Asparagus
2 **cups water**
1$\frac{1}{2}$ **pounds asparagus spears, trimmed**
$\frac{1}{8}$ **teaspoon black pepper (optional)**

1. For sauce, whisk together yogurt, mayonnaise, mustard, lemon juice and salt in small bowl until smooth; set aside.

2. For asparagus, bring water to a boil in 12-inch skillet over high heat. Add asparagus. Return to a boil. Reduce heat; cover and simmer 3 minutes or until crisp-tender. Drain on paper towels.

3. Place asparagus on serving platter; top with sauce. Sprinkle with pepper, if desired.

Makes 6 servings

Peperonata

      1 tablespoon extra-virgin olive oil
      4 red, yellow and/or orange bell peppers, cut into thin strips
      2 cloves garlic, coarsely chopped
     12 pimiento-stuffed green olives or pitted black olives, cut into halves
      2 to 3 tablespoons white or red wine vinegar
     ¼ teaspoon salt
     ¼ teaspoon black pepper

1. Heat oil in large skillet over medium-high heat. Add bell peppers; cook 8 to 9 minutes or until edges begin to brown, stirring frequently.

2. Reduce heat to medium. Add garlic; cook and stir 1 to 2 minutes. *Do not allow garlic to brown.* Add olives, vinegar, salt and black pepper. Cook 1 to 2 minutes or until all liquid has evaporated.   *Makes 4 to 5 servings*

Tip: Peperonata is a very versatile dish. It can be served hot as a side dish or as a condiment with meat dishes. Or, it can be chilled and served as part of an antipasti selection.

Vegetables in Cream Sauce

What You Need
      1 package (16 ounces) frozen broccoli, cauliflower and carrot blend
     ¼ pound (4 ounces) VELVEETA® 2% Milk Pasteurized Prepared Cheese Product, cut into ½-inch cubes
      4 ounces (½ of 8-ounce package) PHILADELPHIA® ⅓ Less Fat Cream Cheese, cubed

Make It
1. LAYER ingredients in microwaveable 1½-quart casserole; cover.

2. MICROWAVE on HIGH 13 minutes or until vegetables are heated through, stirring after 7 minutes; stir.   *Makes 6 servings, ½ cup each*

Prep Time: 10 minutes
Total Time: 23 minutes

Variation: Heat oven to 350°F. Layer ingredients in 1-quart casserole. Bake 55 minutes or until vegetables are heated through; stir.

Artichokes with Lemon-Tarragon Butter

6 cups water
2 teaspoons salt
2 whole artichokes, stems cut off and tips trimmed
¼ cup (½ stick) butter
¼ teaspoon freshly grated lemon peel
2 tablespoons lemon juice
¼ teaspoon dried tarragon

1. Bring water and salt to a boil in large saucepan over high heat. Add artichokes; return to a boil. Reduce heat; cover and simmer 35 to 45 minutes or until leaves detach easily (cooking time will depend on artichoke size).

2. Turn artichokes upside down to drain well.

3. Combine butter, lemon peel, lemon juice and tarragon in small saucepan; bring to a boil over medium-high heat. Serve alongside artichokes.   *Makes 2 servings*

Serving Suggestion: Artichokes also are attractive if cut in half lengthwise before serving.

Red Cabbage and Apples

1 head red cabbage, cored and thinly sliced
3 apples, peeled and grated
¾ cup sugar
½ cup red wine vinegar
1 teaspoon ground cloves
1 cup crisp-cooked and crumbled bacon
    Fresh apple slices (optional)

Slow Cooker Directions
1. Combine cabbage, apples, sugar, vinegar and cloves in slow cooker. Cover; cook on HIGH 6 hours, stirring after 3 hours.

2. To serve, sprinkle with bacon and garnish with apple slices.   *Makes 4 to 6 servings*

Artichokes with Lemon-Tarragon Butter

Creamy Spinach-Stuffed Portobellos

1 tablespoon vegetable oil
1 medium onion, chopped (about ½ cup)
1 medium tomato, chopped (about 1 cup)
1 bag (6 ounces) fresh baby spinach leaves
1 can (10¾ ounces) CAMPBELL'S® Condensed Cream of Celery Soup
    (Regular or 98% Fat Free)
4 large portobello mushrooms, stems removed
2 tablespoons grated Parmesan cheese
1 tablespoon plain dry bread crumbs, toasted

1. Heat the oven to 425°F.

2. Heat the oil in a 10-inch nonstick skillet over medium heat. Add the onion and cook until it's tender-crisp. Add the tomato and spinach and cook just until the spinach is wilted. Stir in the soup and cook until the mixture is hot and bubbling.

3. Place the mushrooms into a 3-quart shallow baking dish. Spoon the spinach mixture into the mushroom caps. Bake for 15 minutes or until the mushrooms are tender.

4. Stir the cheese and bread crumbs in a small bowl. Sprinkle the bread crumb mixture over the mushrooms. Broil 4 inches from the heat until the topping is golden. *Makes 4 servings*

Prep Time: 20 minutes
Bake Time: 20 minutes

tip

To save time, you can buy portobello mushroom caps, with the stems already removed, in the produce section.

Butternut Squash Purée with Maple-Glazed Pecans

Maple-Glazed Pecans
- 1 egg white
- 2 tablespoons maple syrup
- 1 tablespoon firmly packed light brown sugar
- ¼ teaspoon salt
- ¼ teaspoon ground cinnamon
- 2 cups pecans

Butternut Squash Purée
- 1 (2-pound) butternut squash
- 1 tablespoon butter
- 1 shallot, chopped
- 2 tablespoons whipping cream
- 2 tablespoons maple syrup
- ¼ teaspoon salt
- ¼ teaspoon black pepper
- Pinch allspice

1. Preheat oven to 300°F. Line baking sheet with foil; grease foil.

2. For pecans, beat egg white in large bowl until frothy. Add 2 tablespoons maple syrup, brown sugar, ¼ teaspoon salt and cinnamon; beat until well blended. Add pecans; stir until evenly coated. Spread pecans on prepared baking sheet. Bake 30 minutes, turning once or twice. Cool on baking sheet 5 minutes. Stir to prevent sticking; set aside. *Increase oven temperature to 350°F.*

3. Meanwhile, for purée, pierce squash in several places. Microwave 11 to 12 minutes on HIGH or until knife inserted into thickest part comes out easily and squash feels slightly tender to the touch. Set aside until squash is cool enough to handle.

4. Cut squash in half. Scoop out and discard seeds and stringy flesh. Scoop out flesh; place in food processor or blender. Melt butter in small saucepan over medium heat. Add shallot; cook and stir 2 to 3 minutes or until tender. Place in food processor with cream, 2 tablespoons maple syrup, ¼ teaspoon salt, pepper and allspice; process until smooth.

5. Spoon purée into shallow baking dish. Bake 15 minutes to heat through. Sprinkle with ½ cup pecans. Save remaining pecans for another use. *Makes 4 servings*

Cauliflower Tabbouleh

2 packages (12 ounces each) cauliflower florets
3 tablespoons olive oil, divided
1 teaspoon curry powder
1 bunch flat leaf parsley
1 onion, finely chopped
½ seedless cucumber, chopped
1 cup chopped tomato *or* 1 can (about 14 ounces) diced tomatoes, well drained
⅓ cup fresh lemon juice
½ teaspoon black pepper
¼ teaspoon salt

1. Cut large cauliflower florets into uniform pieces. Place cauliflower in food processor or blender; pulse 1 minute or until chopped into uniform granules.

2. Heat 1 tablespoon oil in large nonstick skillet over medium-high heat. Add curry powder; cook until sizzling. Add cauliflower; stir-fry about 10 minutes or until cooked through. Remove from heat and cool.

3. Meanwhile, trim and discard large stems of parsley. Place parsley in food processor; pulse 10 to 20 seconds to chop.

4. Combine cauliflower mixture, parsley, onion, cucumber and tomato in large bowl. Whisk remaining 2 tablespoons oil, lemon juice, pepper and salt in small bowl. Pour over cauliflower mixture; toss well.
Makes 6 servings

Beans and Greens with Curry

1 cup adzuki beans*
4 cups plus 2 tablespoons cold water, plus additional for soaking beans
2 pounds kale or Swiss chard
1 tablespoon extra-virgin olive oil
½ cup diced white onion
2 cloves garlic, minced
2 teaspoons curry powder
¼ teaspoon salt
¼ teaspoon black pepper

*Adzuki beans are small reddish beans with a sweet flavor and high protein content. They are used in Japanese cooking and can be found at natural food markets.

1. Soak beans overnight in enough water to cover by at least 2 inches. Drain beans and rinse well.

2. Place beans in large saucepan with 4 cups water; bring to a boil. Reduce heat and simmer 1 hour or until beans are tender. Drain beans; set aside.

3. Remove stems and ribs from kale and tear into large pieces.

4. Heat oil in large deep skillet over medium heat. Add onion and garlic, cook and stir 5 minutes or until onion is soft and translucent. Add curry powder; cook and stir 30 seconds or until slightly toasted and aromatic.

5. Add kale to skillet. Sprinkle with 2 tablespoons water. Cook 5 minutes or until wilted.

6. Add beans to kale mixture; cook and stir until heated through. Season with salt and pepper.

Makes 6 servings

Savory Spinach with Blue Cheese and Walnuts

1 tablespoon butter
1 large sweet onion, halved and thinly sliced (about 1 cup)
2 cloves garlic, sliced
2 large tomatoes, seeded and chopped (about 3 cups)
¾ cup SWANSON® Chicken Broth (Regular, Natural Goodness® or Certified Organic)
1 bag (11 ounces) fresh baby spinach
Ground black pepper
¼ cup crumbled blue cheese (about 2 ounces)
2 tablespoons chopped walnuts

1. Melt the butter in a 12-inch nonstick skillet. Add the onion and garlic and cook until they're tender, stirring occasionally.

2. Add the tomatoes, broth and spinach. Cook for 2 minutes or until the spinach wilts. Season with the black pepper. Sprinkle with the cheese and walnuts, if desired. *Makes 6 servings*

Prep Time: 15 minutes
Cook Time: 15 minutes

Chili-Rubbed Grilled Vegetable Kabobs

2 ears corn, husked and cut into 1-inch pieces
1 red bell pepper, cut into 12 chunks
1 yellow bell pepper, cut into 12 chunks
1 green bell pepper, cut into 12 chunks
1 sweet or red onion, cut into 12 wedges
2 tablespoons olive oil
1 teaspoon seasoned salt
1 teaspoon chili powder
½ teaspoon sugar

1. Alternately thread corn, peppers and onion onto 12-inch metal skewers. Brush oil evenly over vegetables. Combine seasoned salt, chili powder and sugar in small bowl; sprinkle over all sides of vegetables. Wrap skewers in heavy-duty foil; refrigerate up to 8 hours.

2. Prepare grill for direct cooking. Unwrap skewers; place on grid over medium heat. Grill 10 to 12 minutes or until vegetables are tender, turning occasionally.   *Makes 4 servings*

Herbed Corn on the Cob

1 tablespoon butter or margarine
1 teaspoon mixed dried herbs (such as basil, oregano, sage and rosemary)
⅛ teaspoon salt
Black pepper
4 ears corn (6 to 7 ounces each), husks removed

Microwave Directions
1. Combine butter, herbs, salt and pepper in small microwavable bowl. Microwave on MEDIUM (50%) 30 to 45 seconds or until butter is melted.

2. With pastry brush, coat corn with butter mixture. Place corn on microwavable plate; microwave on HIGH 5 to 6 minutes. Turn; microwave on HIGH 5 to 6 minutes or until tender.
Makes 4 servings

Chili-Rubbed Grilled Vegetable Kabob

Grilled Mesquite Vegetables

2 to 3 tablespoons MRS. DASH® Mesquite Grilling Blend
2 tablespoons olive oil, divided
1 eggplant, trimmed and cut into ½-inch slices
1 zucchini, quartered lengthwise
1 red onion, peeled and halved
2 red bell peppers, cut into large slices
2 green bell peppers, cut into large slices
1 tablespoon balsamic vinegar

Preheat barbecue grill to medium. In large bowl, combine Mrs. Dash® Mesquite Grilling Blend and 1 tablespoon olive oil. Add vegetables and toss until well coated. Place vegetables on grill. Cover and cook, turning vegetables once during cooking, until vegetables are tender and develop grill marks, about 3 to 4 minutes on each side. Remove vegetables from grill as soon as they are cooked. Coarsely chop vegetables into ½-inch pieces. Mix remaining olive oil and balsamic vinegar in large bowl. Add cut vegetables and toss to coat. Serve at room temperature.

Makes 6 servings

Prep Time: 10 minutes
Cook Time: 10 minutes

Note: Grilling vegetables dehydrates them slightly and intensifies the flavors, while Mrs. Dash® Mesquite Grilling Blend adds a third dimension of flavor. This dish makes a colorful accompaniment to any grilled meat.

Creamy Green Beans

8 cups frozen French-cut green beans, thawed and well drained
4 tablespoons (½ stick) butter, divided
2 cups coarsely chopped mushrooms
⅓ cup diced onion
⅓ cup diced celery
⅓ cup grated carrot
2 cups whipping cream
1 cup chicken broth
1 teaspoon salt
½ teaspoon black pepper
½ cup canned French fried onions

1. Preheat oven to 325°F. Place green beans in 2-quart casserole.

2. Melt 2 tablespoons butter in medium saucepan over medium heat. Add mushrooms; cook and stir 2 to 3 minutes or until softened. Transfer to medium bowl.

3. Melt remaining 2 tablespoons butter in same saucepan; add onion, celery and carrot. Cook and stir 5 minutes or until onion is translucent. Stir in cream, broth, salt and pepper; bring to a boil. Reduce heat; simmer 12 to 15 minutes or until mixture thickens slightly. Stir in mushrooms.

4. Pour mushroom mixture over green beans; mix well. Sprinkle with French fried onions; bake 25 minutes or until heated through. *Makes 8 servings*

Cheesy Chile Corn Casserole

1 can (10¾ ounces) CAMPBELL'S® Condensed Cheddar Cheese Soup
¼ cup milk
1 tablespoon butter, melted
   Dash ground red pepper
1 bag (16 ounces) frozen whole kernel corn, thawed
1 can (about 4 ounces) chopped green chiles
1 can (2.8 ounces) French fried onions (about 1⅓ cups)

1. Heat the oven to 350°F. Stir the soup, milk, butter, pepper, corn, chiles and ⅔ **cup** onions in a 1½-quart casserole.

2. Bake for 25 minutes or until the corn mixture is hot and bubbling. Stir the corn mixture.

3. Sprinkle the remaining onions over the corn mixture. Bake for 5 minutes or until the onions are golden brown.   *Makes 6 servings*

Prep Time: 15 minutes
Bake Time: 30 minutes

tip

An oven thermometer is the best way to check how accurately your oven heats. Most are designed to hang on the rack inside the oven to conveniently measure the temperature.

perfect potatoes

Lemon-Mint Red Potatoes

2 pounds new red potatoes
3 tablespoons olive oil
1 teaspoon salt
¾ teaspoon dried Greek seasoning or dried oregano
¼ teaspoon garlic powder
¼ teaspoon black pepper
4 tablespoons chopped fresh mint, divided
1 teaspoon grated lemon peel
2 tablespoons lemon juice
2 tablespoons butter

Slow Cooker Directions

1. Coat 6-quart slow cooker with nonstick cooking spray. Add potatoes and oil; toss to coat. Sprinkle with salt, Greek seasoning, garlic powder and pepper. Cover; cook on LOW 7 hours or on HIGH 4 hours.

2. Stir in 2 tablespoons mint, lemon peel, lemon juice and butter until butter is completely melted. Cover; cook 15 minutes to allow flavors to blend. Sprinkle with remaining 2 tablespoons mint just before serving. *Makes 4 servings*

Prep Time: 25 minutes
Cook Time: 7 hours, 15 minutes (LOW) or 4 hours, 15 minutes (HIGH)

Two-Toned Stuffed Potatoes

3 large baking potatoes (12 ounces each)
2 large sweet potatoes (12 ounces each), dark flesh preferred
3 slices thick-cut bacon, cut in half crosswise diagonally
2 cups chopped onions
⅔ cup buttermilk
¼ cup (½ stick) butter, cut into small pieces
¾ teaspoon salt, divided

1. Preheat oven to 450°F. Pierce potatoes with fork in several places. Bake directly on rack 45 minutes or until fork-tender. Let potatoes stand until cool enough to handle. *Reduce oven temperature to 350°F.*

2. Meanwhile, cook bacon in medium skillet over medium-high heat 6 to 8 minutes or until crisp. Remove from heat; transfer bacon to paper towels.

3. Add onions to drippings in skillet; cook about 12 minutes over medium-high heat or until golden brown. Remove onions from skillet; set aside. Stir buttermilk into skillet, scraping up any browned bits from bottom of pan. Add butter; stir until melted.

4. Cut baking potatoes in half lengthwise with serrated knife; scoop out flesh into large bowl. Reserve skins. Add three fourths buttermilk mixture, ½ teaspoon salt and three fourths onions to bowl. Mash with potato masher until smooth.

5. Cut sweet potatoes in half lengthwise with serrated knife; scoop out flesh into medium bowl. Discard skins. Add remaining buttermilk mixture, ¼ teaspoon salt and one fourth onions to sweet potatoes. Mash with potato masher until smooth.

6. Fill half of each reserved potato skin horizontally, vertically or diagonally with baked potato mixture; fill other half with sweet potato mixture. Top each stuffed potato half with bacon slice. Transfer stuffed potatoes to baking sheet; bake 15 minutes or until heated through.

Makes 6 servings

Note: These stuffed potatoes can be made and frozen weeks in advance. Reheat the frozen potatoes in a preheated 350°F oven for 75 to 90 minutes. If the potatoes are made ahead and refrigerated for a few days, reheat them in a preheated 350°F oven about 25 minutes.

Scalloped Potato-Onion Bake

1 can (10¾ ounces) CAMPBELL'S® Condensed Cream of Celery Soup
    (Regular or 98% Fat Free)
½ cup milk
   Dash ground black pepper
4 medium potatoes (about 1¼ pounds), thinly sliced
1 small onion, thinly sliced (about ¼ cup)
1 tablespoon butter, cut into pieces
   Paprika

1. Stir the soup, milk and black pepper with a whisk or fork in a small bowl. Layer half of the potatoes, half of the onion and half of the soup mixture in a 1½-quart casserole. Repeat the layers. Place the butter over the soup mixture. Sprinkle with the paprika. Cover the dish with foil.

2. Bake at 400°F. for 1 hour. Uncover and bake for 15 minutes more or until the potatoes are fork-tender. *Makes 6 servings*

Prep Time: 10 minutes
Bake Time: 1 hour, 15 minutes

Chive & Onion Mashed Potatoes

2 pounds potatoes, peeled, quartered (about 6 cups)
½ cup milk
1 tub (8 ounces) PHILADELPHIA® Chive & Onion Cream Cheese Spread
¼ cup KRAFT® Ranch Dressing

1. Place potatoes and enough water to cover in 3-quart saucepan. Bring to a boil.

2. Reduce heat to medium; cook 20 to 25 minutes or until tender. Drain.

3. Mash potatoes, gradually stirring in milk, cream cheese spread and dressing until light and fluffy. Serve immediately. *Makes 10 servings*

Prep Time: 10 minutes
Cook Time: 25 minutes

Variation: Substitute KRAFT® Three Cheese Ranch Dressing for Ranch Dressing.

Make Ahead: Mix ingredients as directed; spoon into 1½-quart casserole dish. Cover. Refrigerate several hours or overnight. When ready to serve, bake, uncovered, at 350°F 1 hour or until heated through.

Savory Herb Roasted Potatoes

 2 pounds red potatoes, cut into wedges (about 6 medium)
1⅓ cups *French's*® Cheddar French Fried Onions or *French's*® French Fried Onions
 ¼ cup parsley, minced
 6 cloves garlic, halved
 6 sprigs thyme or rosemary
 2 tablespoons olive oil
 1 teaspoon salt
 ¼ teaspoon ground black pepper
 2 ice cubes
 1 large foil oven roasting bag

1. Toss all ingredients in large bowl. Open foil bag; spoon potatoes into bag in an even layer. Seal bag with tight double folds. Place bag on baking sheet.

2. Place bag on grill over medium-high heat. Cover grill and cook 25 minutes until potatoes are tender, turning bag over once.

3. Return bag to baking sheet and carefully cut top of bag open. Sprinkle with additional French Fried Onions, if desired.   *Makes 4 to 6 servings*

Prep Time: 10 minutes
Cook Time: 25 minutes

Note: Too cold for outdoor grilling? Bake these potatoes in a 450°F oven for 25 to 30 minutes.

Potato-Cauliflower Mash

 3 cups water
 2 cups cubed Yukon Gold potatoes, skin on (about 12 ounces)
10 ounces frozen cauliflower florets
 ¼ cup evaporated milk
 2 tablespoons butter
 ¾ teaspoon salt
 ¼ teaspoon black pepper

1. Bring water to a boil in large saucepan. Add potatoes and cauliflower; return to a boil. Reduce heat; cover and simmer 10 minutes or until potatoes are tender.

2. Drain vegetables; place in blender with evaporated milk, butter, salt and pepper. Blend until smooth, scraping side frequently.   *Makes 4 servings*

Savory Herb Roasted Potatoes

Chunky Ranch Potatoes

3 pounds red potatoes, unpeeled and quartered
1 cup water
½ cup prepared ranch dressing
½ cup grated Parmesan or Cheddar cheese
¼ cup minced chives

Slow Cooker Directions

1. Place potatoes and water in 4-quart slow cooker. Cover; cook on LOW 7 to 9 hours or on HIGH 4 to 6 hours or until potatoes are tender.

2. Stir in ranch dressing, cheese and chives. Use spoon to break up potatoes into chunks. Serve hot or cold.   *Makes 8 servings*

Prep Time: 10 minutes
Cook Time: 7 to 9 hours (**LOW**) or 4 to 6 hours (**HIGH**)

Easy Cheesy Potatoes

What You Need
1 pound russet potatoes (about 4 medium), cut into ½-inch chunks
½ pound (8 ounces) VELVEETA® Pasteurized Prepared Cheese Product, cut up
½ cup chopped onions
¼ cup KRAFT® Real Mayo Mayonnaise
4 slices OSCAR MAYER® Bacon, cooked, drained and crumbled (about ¼ cup)

Make It

1. HEAT oven to 375°F. Combine all ingredients except bacon in 8-inch square baking dish sprayed with cooking spray; cover with foil.

2. BAKE 45 minutes.

3. TOP with bacon; bake, uncovered, 5 to 10 minutes or until potatoes are tender.
                                                                        Makes 10 servings

Prep Time: 15 minutes
Total Time: 1 hour, 10 minutes

Serving Suggestion: Sprinkle with 1 tablespoon chopped fresh parsley just before serving.

Triple Cheese Potato Bake

REYNOLDS WRAP® Non-Stick Foil
2 cans (10¾ ounces each) reduced sodium cream of chicken soup, undiluted
1 container (8 ounces) sour cream
½ teaspoon black pepper
1 package (30 to 32 ounces) frozen hash brown potatoes
¾ cup sliced green onions
1 jar (4 ounces) diced pimientos, drained
¾ cup shredded sharp Cheddar cheese
¾ cup shredded Swiss cheese
¼ cup grated Parmesan cheese

PREHEAT oven to 400°F. Line a 13×9×2-inch baking pan with Reynolds Wrap Non-Stick Foil with non-stick (dull) side toward food; set aside.

COMBINE soup, sour cream and pepper in a large bowl; blend well. Stir in potatoes, onions, pimientos, Cheddar cheese and Swiss cheese. Spoon into foil-lined pan in an even layer; sprinkle with Parmesan cheese.

BAKE 45 minutes to 1 hour or until bubbling and golden brown.

SERVE immediately or cool 25 to 30 minutes; cover with non-stick foil (dull side toward food) and freeze, if desired. *Makes 8 to 10 servings*

Prep Time: 10 minutes
Cook Time: 45 minutes

Reynolds Kitchens Tip: To reheat, thaw covered in refrigerator. Preheat oven to 350°F. Bake 45 minutes to 1 hour or until heated through. Remove foil after 30 minutes heating time.

Blue Cheese Potatoes

2 pounds red potatoes, peeled and cut into ½-inch pieces
1¼ cups chopped green onions, divided
2 tablespoons olive oil, divided
1 teaspoon dried basil
½ teaspoon salt
¼ teaspoon black pepper
2 ounces crumbled blue cheese

Slow Cooker Directions

1. Layer potatoes, 1 cup green onions, 1 tablespoon oil, basil, salt and pepper in slow cooker. Cover; cook on LOW 7 hours or on HIGH 4 hours.

2. Gently stir in cheese and remaining 1 tablespoon oil. Transfer potatoes to serving platter and top with remaining ¼ cup green onions.   *Makes 5 servings*

Prep Time: 10 minutes
Cook Time: 7 hours (LOW) or 4 hours (HIGH)

Potatoes au Gratin

  1½ **pounds red potatoes**
    6 **tablespoons butter, divided**
    3 **tablespoons all-purpose flour**
  ½ **teaspoon salt**
  ¼ **teaspoon white pepper**
1½ **cups milk**
    1 **cup (4 ounces) shredded Cheddar cheese**
    4 **green onions, thinly sliced**
  ¾ **cup cracker crumbs**

1. Preheat oven to 350°F. Spray 1-quart casserole with nonstick cooking spray.

2. Place potatoes in medium saucepan; add enough water to cover potatoes. Bring to a boil over high heat. Cook uncovered, about 10 minutes or until potatoes are still firm in center. Drain; rinse in cold water until potatoes are cool. Drain; set aside.

3. Meanwhile, melt 4 tablespoons butter in medium saucepan over medium heat. Add flour, salt and pepper; stir until smooth. Gradually add milk; stir constantly until sauce is thickened. Add cheese; stir until melted.

4. Cut potatoes crosswise into ¼-inch-thick slices. Layer one third of potatoes in prepared dish. Top with one third onions and one third cheese sauce. Repeat layers twice, ending with cheese sauce.

5. Melt remaining 2 tablespoons butter in same saucepan; stir in cracker crumbs. Sprinkle evenly over top of casserole. Bake uncovered, 35 to 40 minutes or until bubbly and heated through.   *Makes 4 to 6 servings*

Rustic Garlic Mashed Potatoes

2 pounds baking potatoes, unpeeled and cut into ½-inch cubes
¼ cup water
2 tablespoons butter, cut into ⅛-inch pieces
1¼ teaspoons salt
½ teaspoon garlic powder
¼ teaspoon black pepper
1 cup milk

Slow Cooker Directions

1. Combine potatoes, water, butter, salt, garlic powder and pepper in slow cooker; mix well. Cover; cook on LOW 7 hours or on HIGH 4 hours.

2. Add milk to potatoes; mash with potato masher or electric mixer until smooth.

Makes 5 servings

German Potato Salad

10 medium potatoes
1¾ cups SWANSON® Beef Broth (Regular, 50% Less Sodium or Certified Organic)
¼ cup cider vinegar
¼ cup all-purpose flour
3 tablespoons sugar
½ teaspoon celery seed
⅛ teaspoon ground black pepper
1 medium onion, chopped (about ½ cup)
3 tablespoons chopped fresh parsley

1. Place the potatoes into a 4-quart saucepan. Add water to cover. Heat over high heat to a boil. Reduce the heat to low. Cook for 20 minutes or until the potatoes are tender. Drain. Let cool and cut in cubes. Place the potatoes into a large bowl.

2. Stir the broth, vinegar, flour, sugar, celery seed and black pepper in the saucepan. Stir in the onion. Cook and stir over medium-high heat until the mixture boils and thickens. Reduce the heat to low. Cook for 5 minutes or until the onion is tender.

3. Add the parsley and broth mixture to the potatoes and stir to coat. Serve warm.

Makes 12 servings

Prep Time: 15 minutes
Cook Time: 30 minutes

Twice-Baked Potatoes with Sun-Dried Tomatoes

4 large baking potatoes
   Vegetable oil
1 container (16 ounces) sour cream
2 cups (8 ounces) shredded Cheddar cheese, divided
¹⁄₃ cup sun-dried tomatoes packed in oil, drained and chopped
4 tablespoons finely chopped green onions, divided
2 tablespoons butter, softened
1 teaspoon salt
¹⁄₂ teaspoon black pepper

1. Preheat oven to 350°F. Scrub potatoes and pat dry with paper towels. Rub potatoes with vegetable oil; bake 1 hour. Cool 30 minutes.

2. Cut each potato in half lengthwise. Scrape potato pulp into large bowl, leaving ¹⁄₂-inch thick shells. Add sour cream, 1¹⁄₂ cups cheese, sun-dried tomatoes, 3 tablespoons green onions, butter, salt and pepper; mix gently. Fill potato shells.

3. Bake 15 to 20 minutes or until heated through. Top with remaining ¹⁄₂ cup cheese; bake 5 minutes or until cheese is melted. Sprinkle with remaining 1 tablespoon green onions.

Makes 8 servings

Creamy Red Potato Salad

3 pounds red bliss or new potatoes, cut into ³⁄₄-inch chunks
¹⁄₂ cup WISH-BONE® Italian Dressing*
³⁄₄ cup HELLMANN'S® or BEST FOODS® Real Mayonnaise
¹⁄₂ cup sliced green onions
1 teaspoon Dijon mustard
1 teaspoon lemon juice
¹⁄₈ teaspoon ground black pepper

*Also terrific with WISH-BONE® Robusto Italian or House Italian Dressing.

Cover potatoes with water in 4-quart saucepot; bring to a boil over medium-high heat. Reduce heat to low and simmer 10 minutes or until potatoes are tender. Drain and cool slightly.

Combine all ingredients except potatoes in large salad bowl. Add potatoes and toss gently. Serve chilled or at room temperature.

Makes 10 servings

Prep Time: 15 minutes
Cook Time: 10 minutes

Twice-Baked Potatoes with Sun-Dried Tomatoes

Sweet Potato Soufflé

1¼ pounds unpeeled sweet potatoes (about 3 medium)
1 tablespoon butter
¾ cup whipping cream
1 teaspoon salt
¼ teaspoon white pepper
¼ teaspoon ground nutmeg
5 egg whites

1. Place sweet potatoes in medium saucepan; cover with water. Bring to a boil over high heat. Reduce heat and cover. Boil 20 minutes or until fork-tender. Drain; cool to room temperature.

2. Preheat oven to 375°F. Generously butter 1½-quart soufflé dish.

3. Peel sweet potatoes; transfer to large bowl. Add cream, salt, pepper and nutmeg; beat until smooth.

4. Beat egg whites in another large bowl with electric mixer at medium-high speed until stiff peaks form. Gently fold egg whites into potato mixture until well blended.

5. Pour into prepared soufflé dish. Place soufflé dish in 13×9-inch baking pan filled with 1 inch hot water. Bake 1 hour and 10 minutes or until knife inserted into center comes out clean.

Makes 8 servings

Country Scalloped Potatoes

1 can (10¾ ounces) CAMPBELL'S® Condensed Cream of Celery Soup (Regular or 98% Fat Free)
1 can (10½ ounces) CAMPBELL'S® Chicken Gravy
1 cup milk
5 medium potatoes, peeled and thinly sliced (about 5 cups)
1 small onion, thinly sliced (about ¼ cup)
2½ cups diced cooked ham
1 cup shredded Cheddar cheese (about 4 ounces)

1. Stir the soup, gravy and milk in a small bowl. Layer **half** of the potatoes, onion, ham and soup mixture in a 3-quart shallow baking dish. Repeat the layers. Cover the baking dish.

2. Bake at 375°F. for 40 minutes. Uncover and bake for 25 minutes. Top with the cheese. Bake for 5 minutes or until the potatoes are tender and the cheese is melted. Let stand for 10 minutes.

Makes 6 servings

Prep Time: 15 minutes
Bake Time: 1 hour, 10 minutes
Stand Time: 10 minutes

Mashed Potato Layer Bake

4 large white potatoes, peeled, chopped and cooked
2 large sweet potatoes, peeled, chopped and cooked
1 tub (8 ounces) PHILADELPHIA® Chive & Onion Cream Cheese Spread, divided
½ cup BREAKSTONE'S® or KNUDSEN® Sour Cream, divided
¼ teaspoon each: salt and black pepper
¼ cup KRAFT® Shredded Parmesan Cheese, divided
¼ cup KRAFT® Shredded Cheddar Cheese, divided

HEAT oven to 375°F. Place potatoes in separate bowls. Add ½ each of the cream cheese spread and sour cream to each bowl; season with salt and pepper. Mash until creamy.

STIR ½ the Parmesan cheese into white potatoes. Stir ½ of the Cheddar cheese into sweet potatoes. Alternately layer ½ each of the white potato and sweet potato mixtures in 2-quart casserole dish. Repeat layers.

BAKE 15 minutes. Sprinkle with remaining cheeses; bake 5 minutes or until melted.

Makes 14 servings

Prep Time: 25 minutes
Total Time: 45 minutes

Mashed Sweet Potatoes with French Meringue

French Meringue
¾ cup sugar
Pinch salt
4 egg whites
Pinch cream of tartar

Sweet Potatoes
3 cups mashed, hot sweet potatoes (about 2 pounds uncooked)
2 tablespoons crystallized ginger, finely chopped
1 to 2 tablespoons orange juice
1 tablespoon butter, softened

1. Preheat oven 350°F. For meringue, combine sugar and salt in small bowl. Beat egg whites and cream of tartar in large bowl with electric mixer at medium-high speed until soft peaks form. Gradually add sugar mixture to egg whites, beating at high speed until stiff peaks form.

2. For potatoes, combine sweet potatoes, ginger, juice and butter in medium bowl; spread in 2-quart casserole. Spread meringue over sweet potatoes. Bake about 14 to 15 minutes or until meringue is golden. Serve immediately.

Makes 6 servings

**The publisher would like to thank the companies
and organizations listed below for the use of their recipes
and photographs in this publication.**

The Beef Checkoff

Campbell Soup Company

ConAgra Foods, Inc.

Cream of Wheat® Cereal

Delmarva Poultry Industry, Inc.

Del Monte Foods

Dole Food Company, Inc.

Filippo Berio® Olive Oil

The Hershey Company

Kraft Foods Global, Inc.

Mrs. Dash® SALT-FREE SEASONING BLENDS

National Chicken Council / US Poultry & Egg Association

Nestlé USA

North Carolina SweetPotato Commission

Ortega®, A Division of B&G Foods, Inc.

Reckitt Benckiser Inc.

Recipes courtesy of the Reynolds Kitchens

Riviana Foods Inc.

Sargento® Foods Inc.

Unilever

USA Rice Federation®

Veg•All®

metric conversion chart

VOLUME MEASUREMENTS (dry)

⅛ teaspoon = 0.5 mL
¼ teaspoon = 1 mL
½ teaspoon = 2 mL
¾ teaspoon = 4 mL
1 teaspoon = 5 mL
1 tablespoon = 15 mL
2 tablespoons = 30 mL
¼ cup = 60 mL
⅓ cup = 75 mL
½ cup = 125 mL
⅔ cup = 150 mL
¾ cup = 175 mL
1 cup = 250 mL
2 cups = 1 pint = 500 mL
3 cups = 750 mL
4 cups = 1 quart = 1 L

VOLUME MEASUREMENTS (fluid)

1 fluid ounce (2 tablespoons) = 30 mL
4 fluid ounces (½ cup) = 125 mL
8 fluid ounces (1 cup) = 250 mL
12 fluid ounces (1½ cups) = 375 mL
16 fluid ounces (2 cups) = 500 mL

WEIGHTS (mass)

½ ounce = 15 g
1 ounce = 30 g
3 ounces = 90 g
4 ounces = 120 g
8 ounces = 225 g
10 ounces = 285 g
12 ounces = 360 g
16 ounces = 1 pound = 450 g

DIMENSIONS

1/16 inch = 2 mm
⅛ inch = 3 mm
¼ inch = 6 mm
½ inch = 1.5 cm
¾ inch = 2 cm
1 inch = 2.5 cm

OVEN TEMPERATURES

250°F = 120°C
275°F = 140°C
300°F = 150°C
325°F = 160°C
350°F = 180°C
375°F = 190°C
400°F = 200°C
425°F = 220°C
450°F = 230°C

BAKING PAN SIZES

Utensil	Size in Inches/Quarts	Metric Volume	Size in Centimeters
Baking or Cake Pan (square or rectangular)	8×8×2	2 L	20×20×5
	9×9×2	2.5 L	23×23×5
	12×8×2	3 L	30×20×5
	13×9×2	3.5 L	33×23×5
Loaf Pan	8×4×3	1.5 L	20×10×7
	9×5×3	2 L	23×13×7
Round Layer Cake Pan	8×1½	1.2 L	20×4
	9×1½	1.5 L	23×4
Pie Plate	8×1¼	750 mL	20×3
	9×1¼	1 L	23×3
Baking Dish or Casserole	1 quart	1 L	—
	1½ quart	1.5 L	—
	2 quart	2 L	—